TALISA "TALI" LAVARRY

CONFESSIONS FROM YOUR TOKEN BLACK COLLEAGUE

TRUE STORIES AND CANDID CONVERSATIONS ABOUT
EQUITY AND INCLUSION IN THE WORKPLACE

To contact the author or order additional copies:
yourtokenblackcolleague.com

Published by
Yum Yum Morale LLC Publishing House
Seattle, WA

Printed in the United States of America.
First Edition, 2020

Cover design by Anna Dorfman (doorsixteen.com)
Cover photography by Kestrel Bailey (kestrelbailey.com)
Developmental editing by Violet Snow (violetsnowwriter.com)
Copy editing and layout by Nikki Hegstrom (nikkihegstrom.com)

*Some names and identifying details have been changed to protect the
privacy of individuals.*

*The author uses Black and African American interchangeably throughout
the book. She chose to capitalize Black in order to reflect that she is talking
about a group of people and to be consistent with the capitalization of
African American.*

ISBN: 978-1-7345402-0-8 (paperback)
ISBN: 978-1-7345402-1-5 (hardback)
ISBN: 978-1-7345402-2-2 (eBook)

This book is dedicated to my nieces,
Arianna Ethel and Lilyanna Rose.
No matter what you decide to do in life, be true to who you are.
You will know this by what you feel in your gut.
Never waiver.

Acknowledgements

This book has been a long time coming. As I near the end of this journey, I can't help but think that had it not been for a special group of women, I probably wouldn't be here to tell this story. Each of you holds a special place in my heart. You were strangers to each other at the time, yet you found a way to come together in order to stick your noses in my business, create plans for me without my input, and completely ignore my wishes. I chuckle as I think about how furious I was with each of you. I beam from within as I feel a warm sense of gratitude. Anyone who knows me knows that I am the epitome of self-reliant; to find myself in a position where I was unable to care for myself was a foreign concept. I always thought if that should happen, I would surely be on my own. To my team of angels (Chakita, Shaun, Harriet, Nadia, and Amanda) who rescued me on November 10, 2019. Thank you from the bottom of my heart.

To Harriet Bond, my fairy godmother: thank you for seeing me, the part of me that I oftentimes deny to myself. You remind me that I'm beautiful and capable. You allow me to be imperfect. You are always ready and willing to have even the toughest conversations in order to get us through the rough patches. You are honest with me. A great judge of character, you know and trust me. You have never questioned my account of a story or if I was wrong or right in a situation where I told you that I had been mistreated. When I want to celebrate a win, you are there. When I need a shoulder to cry on, you lend me both. The void that you've filled was enormous; when I think of you, when I think of us, I know that there is a God. I know that if you could, you would wave your wand and fulfill my every wish. While you may not have a magic wand, you have a loving heart, a rich soul, and a mind that I feel lucky to have access to. I have been far from perfect throughout my life, and I've fumbled with many relationships. I am grateful that you showed up and even more grateful that you are still here. I love you more than words could say. For being you, thank you.

To Brianna Brookes, my little sister: thank you for always gassing me up. You know your big sister well. I can only hope that I am able to be half of what you see within me. I can imagine that walking in Superwoman's shoes is no easy feat for anyone, but every day of my life I strive to fulfill your grandiose ideals of me. Your name is written countless times in my gratitude journal. Who would have ever thought? To have a sister's love is a gift. A love that is patient, kind, free of envy and boast. There is no pride, not too much rudeness (Lol) and certainly no self-seeking. When it comes to our dynamic, we are no longer easily angered. (Look at God!) We keep no record of wrongdoing. At least, I don't. You better not be keeping any records over there. There is no delight in evil, and we can finally rejoice with the truth. I will always do my best to protect you, and I hope we always strive to trust, even when it's hard. I know that there will always be hope, and with our love we can always persevere. A sisterly love, picked up from the gutter, put back together, dusted off, and stored in a secret place. A love that will never fail.

To Chakita Jefferson, the other pea to my pod, the ying to my yang, my soul mate, my friend in this lifetime since 2004: I know a soulmate when I meet one. There is a much greater bond than what meets the eye. No distance, riff, or obstacle can keep soulmates apart. Even when they have not spoken for a while, each one knows deep within that there is a bond that could never be broken. You've always seen the best in me and have loved and appreciated me from day one. I've done the same when it comes to you. We could talk for hours, and no bystander would be able to articulate the conversation. When we are together, we are our best selves—even when we are not. The sincere love and loyalty between us can be felt by anyone near. A destined friendship that I am grateful for. Thank you for always telling me that it's going to be ok and for taking my advice even when it may be presumed as harsh. You know that I oftentimes know exactly what you need to hear.

Lastly, you know I can't end this without saying that we both know and will always know—that I will NE--------VER find another friend like you. *insider*

To my family, cousin, safe place, friend: I remember years ago, you told me that if you didn't like me you really wouldn't like me, and we both busted out laughing. Those that know and love me have long ago accepted the fact that I can be extra. The thing I appreciate most about you is that you accept me and love me the same no matter what version of myself I present. You've teased me and celebrated me when I was driving a beamer and carrying a Louis bag, and you've picked me up from the airport when I had holes in my pants and not a penny to my name. When I've been on the mountain tops, you've met me there to share a champagne toast to commemorate the moment. When I was in my lowest of lowest valleys, you swooped down, picked me up, and hid me so that no one could see me, and there you held me. You reassured me that I didn't have to do the hardest parts of this life's journey alone. You've fed me, clothed me, and rocked me until I could see the sun again. To know that you are there comforts me. I don't take your love for granted, for even a second. Thank you.

To my mentor Jenefeness Tucker: thank you for being you. You answer when I call, and you make sure that I know that you have my back and that you are willing to help.

Sara Bee Jensen: I'm sure you don't realize how you've upgraded me and the whole nature of this book, and the miles that I foresee it traveling due to your contributions. You are a gem. Sincere in your offerings, and you truly want to see this little Black girl from Louisiana win. You extended your network to me, and for that I am beyond grateful. So many of us know that it isn't what you know, but who you know. I'm so lucky to know you, and while I know you will say that I don't—I owe you!

Kestrel Bailey: you've captured me in ways that have allowed me to shine throughout this process. Your easygoing nature and genuine concern for getting things right has been a breath of fresh air. To think that I was prepared to do it all with my tripod and iPhone. Instead, I've had the pleasure of working with one of the best photographers in the Pacific Northwest. Thank you.

Anna Dorfman: I kid you not, I get chills when I think about how you took my already beautiful cover and put your award-winning touch on it. If someone had told me that my cover would be done by the same artist that has created covers for the likes of Stephen King and Nicholas Sparks, I would have told them that they were being a bit too ambitious, but here we are. For your patience and interest in trying over and over again until I loved it. Thank you.

To my publicist, Nancy Mays: you make me feel like I'm somebody. I love to tease my friends and emphasize the fact that I have a meeting with MY publicist. Thank you for giving me the right to rub you in their faces. You have been dedicated to making sure that I have the most and the best exposure while presenting this book to the world. It's refreshing to have someone on my team that truly cares about positive outcomes.

To my marketing and social media team, Taylor Deering, Alyssa Brown, Angela Kawano, Cheryl "Gigi" Alcedo, Serena Connell, Grace Feyisetan, Melissa Hart, Noah Olberding and Leiah Breit-felder: Thank you all so, so, so much for putting up with me. I am forever indebted to you.

To my contributors, Ryan Hayden, Kristian Ribberström, Colin Stokes, and Terri Swain: you are all professionals with a great deal to lose. The topic of my book could be seen as controversial. I've been shaking in my boots for months as I've anticipated it being released out into the world. Knowing that I have you all there, as the wind beneath my wings, has kept me from changing my mind, ripping up the manuscript, and running away. I truly believe that together, through this work, we will change lives for the better. Thank you, each of you, for believing in me, for trusting me, for partnering with me.

To my writing coach and developmental editor, Violet Snow: we both know that I couldn't have pulled this off without you. You were an answered prayer, more than I imagined I could ever find. You pushed me, you pulled from me. You sat with me as I recalled some of the most painful moments of my life. I will never forget the day you told me that your work and meetings with me would soon be coming to an end. I was shocked to find myself fighting back tears. What an amazing experience it is to share this story with the world. My time spent with you helped me realize how important this topic and my mission is. This is heavy stuff, and you helped me carry it through to the end. Thank you.

To my line editor, Nichelle Hegstrom: you are the best, and I know how lucky I am to have you. You stepped in at the ninth hour, and once we started working together, I understood why I struggled so much to find you. It was all worth it. I couldn't have asked for a person more passionate about words, styles, citations, and all of that stuff you get so technical about. I needed you so much more than I even realized. Thank you from the bottom of my heart.

To Laura Hunt and Loews Hotel 1000 Seattle: you, too, made me feel like I was somebody. Thank you for rolling out the red carpet and welcoming us with open arms during our time spent in your facility for a photo and video shoot. I hope that I am able to spend many more nights there. It was a real treat and allowed me to have some beautiful backdrops.

Danielle Mohlman: I can't forget you. As you have stepped in to help me prepare to someday take this story to a stage, I never dreamed that you would end up being such amazing support for me during the process of writing my book. I feel as though you were my book-writing therapist. When it came to sorting through logistics, troubleshooting, and problem solving, you always allowed yourself to be roped into hearing out my dilemmas while patting me on the back and reminding me of how far I've come. Thank you so much for that.

I could go on and on and on, and I'm sure I've forgotten someone—but I will just say to anyone out there that has contributed to me reaching this goal, THANK YOU! With every part of myself, THANK YOU! From your well wishes, to your compliments, to your offers to help, to your sharing of a post. I am beyond grateful. I have former colleagues that have reached out to encourage me, and people that I've never seen in my life have already expressed gratitude to me. Old friends that have told me they can't wait to buy a copy and new friends that have been cheering me along the way. The bountiful support, even now, has been overwhelming. So much about this process has gone right that I know I am exactly where I am supposed to be. If you've ever experienced this feeling, you know and understand just how grateful I am.

Thank You

Preface

Young, Cute, and Skinny should have been the name of the continuing education program I attended to earn my certification in meeting and event planning. The accelerated summer session, with classes held every day including weekends, allowed me to acquire credentials in several weeks that some people would spend months or even years pursuing. The fee, which I could not afford at the time, had been waived. I felt extremely fortunate.

Prior to the certification, I had just finished four years of working as a buyer. During that time, I was passed over for a position I should have been next in line for, I lost my office due to an act of microaggression by the white, male director, and I was forced to view stiletto ballbusting porn whenever I entered the office of the company's attorney. Finally, I packed up my entire life, loaded it on a U-Haul, and moved from Texas to San Francisco.

I saw event management with a reputable corporation or organization as a dream job, and I was excited to find a program that seemed tailored just for me. I wasn't surprised to find that I was the only Black woman in the class.

Towards the end of the program, I told the instructor I wanted to work as a pharmaceutical meeting or corporate event planner. She looked at me with pity in her eyes and said, "Dear, the only place I've ever seen them hire Black gals is over at the LaQuinta Inn." My classmates gasped. She shook her head. "It's just the truth. I'd hate to tell you any different and have you out there searching and networking, only to get frustrated when you realize you're fighting an uphill battle. I almost wish I could warn you gals before you sign up for this course."

A slender Asian woman behind me asked, "Would that be an issue for me as well?"

"Oh, no dear, you're young, you're cute, and you're skinny. You gals can walk right in to practically any corporate office you want and get hired."

Several students pulled me to the side later that day to apologize and say how mortified they'd felt by her remarks.

Our last day of class was on a Saturday. By Wednesday, I was working as an event manager for one of the most reputable governmental and business organizations in both the city and the country.

Then the real challenges began.

Why I Wrote This Book

Since the election of Donald Trump as President of the United States and the protests resulting from the murder of George Floyd by a white policeman, the term post-racial has disappeared from public discourse. But when I started working in the corporate world in 2004, the US was in a state of amnesia. Four years later, the election of our first Black president, Barack

Obama, lulled us with a sense of progress. When the pendulum swung back in 2016, the veneer that had cloaked racism from view was torn away, exposing ugly truths.

After years of seeking resolution for the troubling issues I faced in the business world, I came to realize that those with the power to address corporate racism are blinded by their own biases. They refuse to entertain the idea that they might be contributing to and perpetuating an environment that is far from inclusive. I also realize that once someone is willing to admit their own bias, they have the potential to open their hearts and deepen their understanding, while creating an environment that benefits both their minority employees and their business as a whole.

According to a study by the National Opinion Research Center at the University of Chicago, Black people represent less than 1 percent of Fortune 500 CEOs, and Blacks currently make up 10 percent of college graduates.[1] A just society would have nurtured and hired 50 Black CEOs among those companies. Instead, the research found only four: at the head of Lowe's, TIAA, Merck & Co., and Tapestry.

Only 3.2 percent of executives and senior manager-level employees are African American. On average, 58 percent of Blacks have indicated they experience racism in their jobs, with participants from the Midwest reporting the highest rate at 79 percent, and the Northeast the lowest at 44 percent.[2]

This book is about so much more than sharing a few sad stories. I'm convinced that after reading the stories presented in this book, you will agree that I have been called to do this work.

While researching people who have made activism and equity their call of duty, I envisioned them as forthright, radical, and courageous. I've always rejected the notion that I'm bold or outspoken, in the workplace or elsewhere. I simply wanted to go to work, play by the rules, and be self-sufficient while living an honorable, healthy, and happy life. In hindsight, I realize that despite my desire to fly under the radar, my friends would tell you that I have a strong personality. It's embedded in me. When life presents options, I never take the easy way out or leave things unsaid. A therapist once told me that there are few people in the world that function in this way.

Just by being myself, I tend to force others to recognize their shortcomings or their propensity to do what's easy, rather than what's right.

I've learned that for some, this can come across as intimidating or offensive. My desire to perfect things can come at the most inconvenient time for others. In my attempt to go along to get along, I've tried to focus on the progress we've made as a country, but my deep frustration has never allowed me to yield. At this point, I am compelled to place myself in a position that allows me to speak up in favor of more progressive change. Although I'm afraid to be vulnerable and outspoken on the sensitive topic of racism, I'm even more afraid not to.

My Goals

While I love the idea of validating others who have found themselves in my position, that is not my ultimate goal in writing this book. Yes, I want to help Black women who are mistreated, overlooked, and played against each other every day in corporate America. We are judged harshly, often for things that we have no control of. I'm no stranger to fighting for myself when I've done absolutely nothing wrong. I've worked ten times harder than my colleagues, only to find myself being coached in regard to how I need to be and do better. When I've been wrongly accused, my defenses were dismissed. I've been warned that I shouldn't attempt to defend myself because it labels me as an uncoachable troublemaker. This attitude has placed me in countless lose-lose situations.

While I know my stories will ring true for many Black women, and it is my honor to be affirmative, my real goal is to place these stories and sentiments in the laps of those who refuse to acknowledge the failure of corporate America to truly provide equality for minority groups. I hope those who belong to more advantaged groups will find themselves curious about the invisible burden we carry as we come into your offices day after day, month after month, and year after year. Most of the time we feel isolated, ostracized, and oppressed.

I believe each of us has a role to play in promoting inclusion, not only in the workplace but in our day-to-day lives. I want to contribute to the much needed and ongoing dialogue about diversity, equality, and inclusion in the workplace. Most importantly, I hope to inspire leaders such as yourself, who hold the power within your organizations. You have a tremendous potential to initiate and demand positive change. I hope my accounts of discrimination and abuse will motivate you to do more than just talk about the need for change, and to actually take action to get to the root of the issue. Make it nonnegotiable for the company you lead to systematically take actions that will not only benefit those that are currently oppressed but will benefit the organization and ultimately, the nation as a whole.

This book consists of three intertwining threads: Stories, Confessions, and Conversations. The Stories are accounts of my experience in corporate America, of struggling to deal with the racism that undermines minorities' ability to succeed even in companies supposedly devoted to diversity and inclusion. The Confessions are my observations of the problematic components and attitudes that we need to examine if progress is going to be made toward real diversity and inclusion in the workplace. The Conversations are based on my interviews with people I call allies—white professionals who use their power to counteract racism in business by finding and implementing solutions that have transformed company environments.

The stories in this book are real. However, with the exception of the conversations with white allies, I have changed the names of people and places in order to protect myself and others.

Contents

Introduction:

I Left a Piece of My Heart at Chuck E. Cheese

The name I was given at birth is Talisa Shenece Lavarry. Four years ago, I adopted the pen name Tali Love. This name exemplifies my personal brand and ardent spirit, and the shortening of Talisa has proven to be more ethnically ambiguous, easier to pronounce, and more acceptable in corporate America. According to a survey conducted by McKinsey, 25.5 percent of resumes received callbacks if African American candidates' names were made to sound white. Only 10 percent received a callback if they did not alter their names.[3]

I'm somewhat ashamed to admit that only recently have I accepted how prevalent racism still is in this country. In recent months, I've had a number of conversations with Blacks who were born, like me, in the 1980s, and all of us agree that the era contributed to our miscalculation of the degree of inequality we would have to face as we came of age. In the 80s, civil rights initiatives were at a point where they appeared to be flourishing and moving in a positive direction: by the late 60s, Blacks had achieved access to fair housing. In the early 70s, Black women created their own branch of the burgeoning feminist movement and created an African American women's movement. Representative Shirley Chisholm of New York became the first African American candidate and the first female candidate to run for president of the United States as a part of a major party.

There were defeats as well. In June 1978, in the case of *Regents of the University of California v. Bakke*, the US Supreme Court ruled that the use of strict racial quotas was unconstitutional;[4] however, the fact remained that institutions of higher education could rightfully use race as a criterion in admissions decisions in order to ensure diversity. While the courts used these kinds of decisions to limit the scope of affirmative action programs over the next decade, many people in the Black community viewed this progress as a win.

So, by the time the 80s rolled around, Blacks were proud of all that had been accomplished, and we found ourselves positioned to be treated with more respect and fairness than ever before. We were becoming college educated, we were making waves in the political arena, and we were finding our way into some of the top companies in the nation. We were a hit on the basketball courts and football fields, and the nation's biggest talk show host, Oprah Winfrey, looked like us. On top of that, the white people didn't only embrace her—they seemed to love her. It's no wonder I grew up with the false notion that we were "free at last."

My beginnings, in northern Louisiana, were humble, and much of my childhood was tumultuous. My parents were high school sweethearts who married when my mother was seventeen and pregnant. When I was little, she worked at Chuck E. Cheese, and I was allowed to go to work with her. The staff and customers doted on me, and I basked in the attention. I think I was about about five years old or so when she found a better job as a secretary. There, I couldn't tag along, eat pizza, or play with fun characters. It was a win for Mama but a huge loss for little me.

My father was a maintenance man and an amateur boxer accustomed to using physical force; it may come as no surprise that he also used it to solve personal problems, which sadly included how he dealt with me. While other girls my age were known as *Princess* to their fathers, mine decided to assign me the nickname *Ugly*. As I ducked and dodged his unpredictable rage, my mother kept her head placed firmly beneath the sand. I learned early on that if I cried out for help, there was a pretty good chance that no one would come to my rescue. In fact, it was risky even expressing my needs. I would have to weigh the risks versus the potential reward, so I often failed to articulate what I wanted. Having my needs unmet or finding a way to fulfill them on my own became my norm.

For as far back as I can remember, I have been a person who has persevered in the midst of storms. With limited support and resources, I've always managed to find a way to learn, create, and aspire to be and have more. Much of this talent was developed as a result of constantly seeking ways to hear "I'm proud of you," "You're beautiful," "You can call on me," "I care about you," and "I love you." I longed to feel the warmth of those words.

Without the support of my parents, I successfully worked my way through college. I graduated with honors and promptly found a job as a purchasing manager for two stores on a riverboat casino in my hometown. When I left, I tried my hand at a few other purchasing roles but felt unfulfilled. In the midst of drunk nights out, dysfunctional relationships, and throwing money down the drain, one of the biggest lessons I learned was that my background and upbringing had been a foundation for the woman I was becoming. I discovered the world of self-help and personal development and began to nurture myself with books like *Who Moved My Cheese?* by Spencer Johnson, MD, *Think and Grow Rich* by Napoleon Hill, and *Will I Ever Be Good Enough?* by Karyl McBride, PhD, to name a few.

Those early years of my adult life were bittersweet. The more I learned, the more I believed that I needed to learn more. I always felt as though I couldn't learn enough, fast enough. I also felt like I was constantly finding things that I needed to change about myself. For a number of years, I was a self-help addict. I would anxiously reach toward more and more content in hopes that the next book, video, or magazine article would reveal all that was wrong with me and how to finally fix myself. I felt so lucky to even realize that a self-help genre existed. Where I'm from, people would operate on autopilot with the belief that life just happened to them, rather than the knowledge that we are in control of so much as it relates to the circumstances and outcomes of our lives. Discovering this reality was the sweet part. Realizing the magnitude of my own brokenness was the bitter part.

Before settling into a secure awareness of myself through my search for clarity, I was beset by my ignorance, the lack of love and support from my family, and the dark religious beliefs that were a staple in the South. I felt pretty crappy inside. By acknowledging my feelings and their sources, I started on a journey of deep emotional healing.

I share my past to show that I am fully aware I wasn't given the best foundation to thrive in some of the positions I've held throughout my career. So many times, I've been impaired by the imposter syndrome, trembling inside as I offered up my services alongside white women who had devoted husbands, men who reminded them of their fathers. Having been estranged from my family for the majority of my adult life, I've had to deal with circumstances that most of the people around me couldn't relate to. For years, I was torn between appearing aloof by sparing my colleagues the details of my jagged emotional foundation or potentially being judged by sharing the truth of who I was and where I came from.

Luckily, as I've matured and learned more about life and people, I have found the courage and the space to be forthcoming about my beginning, my present, and what I aspire to reach in the future. This freedom comes partly from having taken an issue I'm passionate about and making it my life's work.

I am the founder of a diversity, equity, and inclusion consultancy called Yum Yum Morale. In my practice, I work with organizations to create and nurture work environments that are sustainable for marginalized groups of people. I've discovered that the majority of Black people have had to build up parts of ourselves from feeble infrastructures and more than likely have experienced some very challenging circumstances long before we entered the workforce.

The systemic roots of racism in our country run deep and penetrate areas far above and beneath the challenges we face at work. These roots cross and infiltrate families, generation after generation. From minimal access to healthcare, to the frequent denial of capital, to lack of awareness regarding opportunities for education, the African American race is at a disadvantage. We are seeing the evidence that Black lives have not seemed to matter in this country, although life is the ultimate human right. Protestors and activists have dared to call out the ongoing disparity under the shadow of white America. Space has recently been made for many of us to express our sentiments and share our stories.

As I witness companies setting aside budgets to devote to the abolishment of systemic racism, I am optimistic. No doubt there will be setbacks, but now, more than ever, the ground is fertile and ready for the cultivation of change. People are ready to absorb the disturbing stories of so many African Americans who have spent years kicking and screaming in an attempt to survive. I hope these stories will move people and motivate them in the direction of change.

These days, I am allowing myself to believe I can thrive. I want to nurture a better world for the next generation, one that allows them to be free of guilt or shame about not having the same foundation and access to resources as their colleagues.

Through my work, I teach business leaders and every member of their workforce the importance of getting to know one another on a human level. We have to engage with each other in a way that allows every person to be imperfect. The awareness that marginalized people deal with an extra layer of concerns allows you to see how it impacts their day-to-day. For example, something as simple as their ride to work or going to a certain establishment or part of town may cause more stress than you can imagine. As we come to understand each other, we learn to work together in mutual support.

I'd like to show you what work was like for one particular corporate employee, and I know many Black women and other marginalized people have similar incidents to recount. In this book I am confessing some of my most personal and humiliating experiences and thoughts regarding the crippling inequality I've dealt with for years. I hope it opens your eyes and shifts your perspective.

1

I Confess

My internal dialogue can be moody. Sometimes it's upbeat and positive, other times critical and disparaging. No matter which, there's no escaping it. The antagonist within was at her loudest when I hit rock bottom.

◆

Time after time, job after job, it's been the same story. Not only was I there telling you which way to go, you had therapists saying you were submitting yourself to toxic levels of mental manipulation. And then you thought it was smart to add a man to the mix? I tried to warn you. Why on earth would any man love you? You're not even good at loving yourself. Every day, year in and year out, you went into offices and work environments that didn't accommodate you. You pretended to be someone else, hoping to have a life outside of the one that was truly meant for you. For decades now, you've tried to master the art of censoring yourself, hiding the essence of who you are. You've changed everything: hair, clothes, tone of voice, mannerisms, hand gestures, accent. You even gave yourself a new name. But you didn't really change. You are Black. Dark skin, full lips, kinky hair. That doesn't sound very corporate, does it? But it does sound real. Over the next few days, I suggest you take this time to get real. You need to truly think about and accept the reality of where you belong versus where you are simply not welcomed.

Startled by loud pounding on the door, I rolled my eyes and let out a deep sigh. Staying in the bathroom too long is cause for concern in a psychiatric hospital. The charge nurse that was on duty at the time seemed to be obsessed with exerting his authority and keeping me on an extremely tight rope.

"Hey Tali! What are you doing?" Knock, knock, knock. "Hey, do you hear me? Don't make me send someone in there!"

"I'm washing my face if that's okay with you."

"Look, you don't gotta be a smart ass about it. Hurry up and come out. You've been in there long enough."

After more than a decade of positioning myself as the token Black within corporate America, here I was in this strange place, under constant supervision. I was trapped and couldn't escape. I just wanted to spend some time away from all the noise. I craved a moment to myself, even if it was in a tiny and questionably muggy bathroom. I needed time to collect my thoughts and reflect on how I ended up there in the first place.

Only then, after unravelling a very complex, confusing, and perhaps inevitable series of events, did I realize how much I'd hurt myself. Not only had I hurt myself, I willfully allowed so many others to hurt me. As a result of these experiences, I have decided to share a few confessions.

The Purpose and Practice of Confession

A traditional practice of Catholicism: *Confessions* offer a time and space to relive and share stories, incidents, images, thoughts, interactions, and reactions. Having the willingness to confess signifies a belief that one has sinned. The practice evolved into a process of individual confession after which a spiritual leader would assign an appropriate penance and offer a prayer of absolution. This sacred practice was their way of seeking true forgiveness while reestablishing their bond with the community. This ritual was designed to restore sinners and make them whole again.

The Process of Confession

The practice begins with a thorough examination of one's own conscience. Through the lens of the Ten Commandments, the Beatitudes, and other scriptures, the sinner admits the error committed and accepts the need to make amends, with a firm resolve not to take part in such action or thought again.

After expressing these convictions, the person receives from the priest a penance, an act that serves as an outward expression of repentance for having done wrong. Examples of penance are the commitment to offer up a specific prayer or series of prayers, a financial or verbal offering to those offended, a sacrifice, or a service rendered. The goal is to make whole what has been broken.

Confessions From Your Token Black Colleague

In the 1990s, South Africa's Truth and Reconciliation Commission helped a divided society with a violent past work through that past and move forward. In a similar way, I propose using the metaphor of confession as a tool to help abolish the systemic structure of racism in the United States. Out of respect for the customs of the Catholic community, and in order to simplify the solutions I'm suggesting, I've made adaptations. Each of the Confession chapters of this book will end with a Proposal for Atonement and Reconciliation. While not taking the role of an actual priest, I am holding space for those who are ready to make thorough audits of themselves, their thoughts, and their behaviors during interactions with Blacks and other minorities in the workplace. It is my hope that experiencing these stories and confessions through my eyes will not only transform you, but motivate you to prioritize the need for change within your organization. Your self-reflection and commitment to making these changes are vital to the positive transformation that is so desperately needed in this country and in this world.

Within the faith, the first confession is nerve-wracking, requires a great deal of preparation, and serves as a foundation for potential future confessions and healing.

My First Confession Is Owed to Myself

For the sake of this analogy, I ask that you view the myriad of offenses that I present in this book as sins and the people who have committed them as sinners. For each of the chapters titled "Confession," I describe the transgressions of the oppressors while suggesting how they might confess their "sins." Then I offer my heartfelt attempt to define their errors and offer solutions that will begin to heal the wounds of those who have been battered and bruised by oppressors in the workplace.

Black men and women alike suffer on their jobs. Other marginalized groups of people suffer as well. My confessions and stories are told from the viewpoint of a Black woman. I know the complexities of our battles, from fighting for our sanity to coping with the race and gender wage gaps woven into the fabric of the complex American culture. When we gather our courage to challenge these conditions, our arguments are swept under the rug. The white people who have the power to make changes are typically afraid to broach the topic of race. I believe they realize the problem is enormously complex and fear that if they admit its existence, they will be required to fix a situation that feels overwhelming and unfixable. People are more comfortable discussing gender wage gaps, but the focus on this issue distracts from the experience of Black women at work. I am committed to learning all I can and sharing it with the expectation that the message will fall on the ears of someone who cares enough to address these issues—which I believe are fixable.

I understand the discomfort and the work involved in uprooting long-standing systems and behaviors. But through education, communication, solidarity, and empathy, we can work together to change the narrative and current conditions for Black women and other marginalized groups in corporate America and in the nation as a whole.

Starting with Me

I am ashamed to admit that in my ignorance some part of me believed that tokenism was a virtue. I told myself that I was a better and a more accepted version of Black. There are many Blacks in America who both subconsciously and consciously walk around with this belief. Sadly, it not only works against the individual, but it also works against us as a whole. This way of thinking only adds to the institutional racism that so many of us are fighting to abolish.

Wikipedia defines *tokenism* as: "the practice of making a perfunctory or symbolic effort to fulfill a requirement, especially by recruiting a small number of people from underrepresented groups in order to give the appearance of equality within a workforce."

There is so much work to be done toward abolishing white supremacy, and while the concept begins with the word white, we, the black colleagues, have to take ownership for feeding into it. We have subconsciously bought into ideas that have been deeply rooted deep in the history of slavery, including that Black women are supposed to work hard and not complain. After the end of official slavery, most Black women had no choice but to work, usually in low paying jobs. There has been progress at correcting the practice of offering the highest paying jobs to white men while discriminating against women. However, Black women are still subject to the remnants of the historical narrative that devalued our worth and contribution to the workforce.

Long-standing stereotypes have also contributed to unethical standards and practices. The Black woman is seen as angry and negative. She is intimidating and always has a chip on her shoulder. Being aware of these assumptions, I tried hard to counteract them, repressing my natural reactions in many situations. As for the idea that Black women are resistant to hard work and have to be pushed to perform well, I know from my own experience that this stereotype couldn't be further from the truth. There is also a damaging consensus that Black women should be satisfied and grateful to have any job rather than feeling entitled to what they might consider the best one.

Every day, many of us are getting up to go into an office to play a game that was never designed for us to have any possibility of winning. My idea of winning was to be invited into the room. Little did I know I was being used in order to give the impression that the companies I worked for were compliant when it came to offering equal opportunities to applicants. But when you know better, you do better. It's time for me to forgive myself.

My Proposal for Atonement and Reconciliation

Dearest Talisa,

Your exodus from the corporate world was one of the hardest experiences of your life. Your sanity was threatened, and your life was emptied of meaning. You couldn't find a reason within or outside of yourself to go on. A perfect storm of events forced you into a space where you had to look deep within and search yourself through and through. For years you had looked for ways to adapt to hostile environments by changing parts of yourself. You shouldered much of the blame for the treatment you received. You sacrificed your dignity and your pride.

There were reasons for what you did. Ill-informed, working with limited resources and without loving support, you did the best you could with what you had. Your exodus led you to the rockiest region of rock bottom so you could finally see your experiences for what they truly were. You learned lessons and can finally see the bigger picture. Every lost opportunity, every bit of praise you were deprived of, every rejection, and every failed relationship has prepared you for this moment.

Like all effective forms of penance, your assignment is not a punishment but a path toward redemption and an opportunity to right your wrongs. Your task is to love and trust yourself. Share your story, with stringent honesty and a heart devoted to service. You are expected to take the knowledge you have acquired and the connections you have made and utilize them for the good of Black women and marginalized groups of people all over the country and the world.

Your contribution will open hearts and transform minds, paving the way for the new generation and creating a world of increased opportunity for all of us.

2
Hidden Figure

I was never officially acknowledged or given credit for one of the most poignant initiatives of my career. As a result, I still find myself hesitating to mention it today.

Ileapt over, dodged, and battled to demolish barrier after barrier in my quest to diversify a San Francisco organization that hired me but gave me no support. My initiative succeeded, against all odds. Sadly, I was denied any opportunity to claim it as my own.

From the start, the only marketing rep that I had access to refused to assist me, and her boss let her get away with supporting me less than she did others. My newly assigned direct report, an older white woman, reluctantly informed me that she'd overheard a conversation that led her to believe that the marketing rep didn't want to work with me because I was a Black woman. She apologized on her behalf and said that she wished there was something that she could do, but her hands were tied.

With no other options, I resorted to doing much of it myself.

I drafted a plan, including a mission statement, objectives, monetization, logo, and structure. The program would be announced with a launch party, to create buzz and set the foundation for a huge local movement.

I requested a meeting with leadership and submitted my proposal. They responded that someone had previously put together a similar project but had been too busy to see it through, and they would get back to me with a decision and what my allotted budget would be. Eventually they said I could move forward, but I had no budget; I should go ahead and plan what I could, and hopefully there would be a budget in time to bring it to fruition.

I recruited a board to assist me with the initiative, including fundraising. The owner of a huge, trendy-looking building was willing to host the event for free. I found a DJ who was excited about the cause, and he offered his service pro bono, as well. He even threw in the equipment and staff that allowed us to host a separate silent disco lounge, which happened to be a fairly new party trend and all the rage at that time. I negotiated with a local signage company, and they donated a free step-and-repeat banner that I used for leverage in my sponsorship proposals for other things that I needed. I even found a photographer that agreed to set up a photo booth with on-demand printing capabilities and huge variety of fun props. To top it off, a dozen or so food and drink vendors agreed to set up shop throughout the large building and offered free samples to all of the attendees.

A few days before the event, it became evident that I was actually going to pull this off, and without a doubt, it would be a huge deal. I'd been ignored by management up to this point, and all meeting requests to discuss my progress had been declined. My colleagues acknowledged that I'd had almost no support, to an astounding degree. Yet they didn't seem able or interested in speaking up for me, although many of them did offer to carry supplies to the venue and help me set up.

The event was a groundbreaking, game changing hit. It was just what the outdated, white-male-dominated organization needed. On that day, one of my newly recruited board members walked me to the door and said, "Look." I became teary-eyed as I saw a line of young and diverse people wrapped around the building, waiting to get into an event that I created from nothing. Despite the many attempts to starve me and stop me at every turn, I actually pulled it off. I could not believe it. *I did it.*

My colleagues congratulated and hugged me, expressing their admiration at what I was able to accomplish, despite the resistance and adversity I'd faced. I looked around at the dancing, partying, happy crowd of various ages and races. I was proud; the moment felt surreal after all the struggle and angst. My thoughts were interrupted by a thump on the microphone.

To my surprise, the president of the organization was trying to get the attention of everyone in the room. There he was, standing on the stage—announcing the initiative, how excited he was about it, how much he knew that the organization needed more diversity, and how hard the office had worked to pull it all together.

I was floored. From the looks on my colleagues' faces, I could tell they were floored too. I began rationalizing, *Okay, it makes perfect sense that he would be here and that he would speak. I did try to work with him on this, so he knew about it. I'm sure he was just busy. It's good that he's putting his stamp on it.*

I positioned myself to join him on the stage.

He never even looked my way. He received the audience's applause and waved as he walked away.

Pathetically, in a panic and in an attempt to gain some form of recognition for all of my hard work, I asked a board member to go on stage and acknowledge me as their leader. She accepted the task, and I pretended to be surprised.

Colored Invisible

The following week, the president called a celebratory happy hour and meeting for the staff at a local bar. There, he talked about how well the launch had gone and how proud he was of all the work that had gone into it. He looked over at one of my colleagues, a middle-aged white man that worked in the sales and membership growth department. "So tell us, Dillion, what are your takeaways from the event, and what would you have done differently if you could go back and do it again?"

Dillion and the rest of the team looked confused and uncomfortable. They all glanced at me. Dillion hesitated and then replied, "I thought it was amazing, and everyone seemed to really enjoy it. I don't think I would change a thing."

"Well, you should be proud of the work you've done. What are your plans moving forward?" Dillion shifted in his seat. "I didn't have anything to do with this. It was all Talisa's work. We were just there to support her."

The president was visibly deflated. He scanned the room for support, but everyone was nodding in agreement with Dillion's response. Finally, he grudgingly acknowledged me. With a sneer in his voice, he asked me, "So what was your takeaway from the event?"

Hiding my devastation, I replied, "It was the highlight of my career. I presented an idea at an embryonic stage and saw it come to fruition. My goal was to diversify the company, and this plan set us on a realistic path to do so. And we've only just begun." I was satisfied with my answer and proud of myself for maintaining my composure.

The president glared at me. "I have a problem with you saying 'I'." Nothing here is done alone. We work as a team. You couldn't have done any of this without the team that sits here before you."

You could hear a pin drop in the room as we all sat, stiff and uncomfortable. He clearly wanted me to cower and retract my statement. I refused. I sat and looked at him. He would have to make the next statement.

"Well, I'd like to buy you all a drink to celebrate your success," he said finally. "Waiter, can you assist us please?" I could see the remorse on my colleagues' faces.

As the waiter approached, I grabbed my handbag and coat and stood up. "If this meeting is over, I'm going to have to excuse myself. I have a prior obligation that I must attend to." Dillion stood up to say that he had to leave as well, and two female colleagues joined us. This left the president there with two newer employees, one who worked the front desk and the other was an intern. He looked dumbfounded as we walked out.

I was never given credit for creating a board and a network of young professionals who diversified the organization and continues to thrive to this day. After the way I'd been treated, I had to find another place to work. Unfortunately, I suffered many of the same injustices at the next job.

3

An Urgent Confession

While we are all forced to participate in the games of office politics; it is a very defeatist position for a Black woman to be in. Many would argue that white men in America write the rules, manage the courses, and call all the plays. They are trusted to lead organizations and are in key positions to make positive change. I believe that at this moment in time, the onus shouldn't be placed on the underdogs to pull themselves up. The onus is on white men in power to create work environments that are both inclusive and sustainable for marginalized people.

To the white, male CEOs and business leaders that I've encountered during my professional career, this is my confession to you.

I'd like to welcome you to this dialogue, and while I consider these confessions acts of penitence, I am fully aware that the offenses that have been committed do not belong to me. Neither is it my duty to right the wrongs or disclose my experiences as a sacrament of penance. I do, however, have hope of absolution. In order to do so, I must begin with you. We need your attention if we are to truly initiate and nurture the intrinsic changes necessary to heal our wounds, forge a new path, and reconcile our protracted and convoluted history. I humbly present myself to you in pursuit of bringing your awareness to these issues. I deem myself, my story, and my mission worthy.

You See Me

You've shown me time and time again that you are fully aware of my power. You've complimented me on my ability to think outside of the box. You've gone out of your way to recruit me, then you've thrown me into a nest of vipers, closed the door to your corner office, and left me to fend for myself.

I've had countless witnesses who have consoled me while assuring me that the problem wasn't me. What I haven't had is people who felt comfortable telling *you* what they had seen.

Good Cop Bad Cop

Spouting clichés and checking off boxes isn't enough. Telling HR to handle it while protecting your company and your assets isn't enough. We don't want handouts, and we don't need anyone to walk on eggshells with us. We do need you to realize and admit that we are treated unfairly within the organizations that you are held responsible for.

This isn't about my inability to make the cut and stay the course. This is about the fact that my presence alone has the potential to make my colleagues uncomfortable. This unfortunate fact gives me the unspoken task of trying to figure out who I need to pretend to be in order to keep them from going on the defensive.

with the responsibility to assimilate and fit into a culture our white colleagues have created and continue to safeguard. Our double bind struggle to fit in while also being true to ourselves shouldn't hinder our ability to contribute to your business objectives.

My Proposal for Atonement and Reconciliation

My call to action goes well beyond asking you to pressure your recruiting team to hire a couple of token employees. That's easy, and you've been doing that for years. My call to action is that you dig deeper and place focus on making the work environment sustainable for the minorities you introduce to your team. I'm challenging you to refrain from the habitual practice of listening only to the jaded opinions of people that you are more familiar with. Consider that, although you may be under the impression that your employees have strong ethics, morals and values, there is a possibility that they may not be telling you the entire truth when speaking about the performance or demeanor of minorities. Furthermore, I challenge you to accept that racism, ageism, ableism, classism, sizeism, homophobia, etc. are real and shaping the semblance of your organization. Accepting this fact does not mean that the people you work with and trust are bad people. It simply means that many of them are naive, fearful, and more comfortable with pointing fingers at the innocent than they are with facing and addressing their own unconscious and damaging biases.

Change begins with you. Only you can set the standard to create an environment where everyone feels welcome. Every member of your workforce should know that in order to be a part of your

It's not easy, what I'm asking you to do. I'm not saying there's a simple solution. I am saying that your acknowledgement is crucial for people such as myself. Despite the persistent narratives about people who look like me, we don't deserve the treatment we have to endure when pursuing our career goals.

How long will you continue paying lip service to diversity and inclusion while allowing xenophobia and ethnocentrism to dominate the culture of your company? While we're at it, let's talk about culture—a popular buzzword in today's corporate world.

Company Culture Is Problematic

Culture influences how a company operates and how its employees experience their work. Different definitions of culture include elements such as: ideas, customs, social behavior, values, attitude, and atmosphere. The word culture derives from the word cultivation, as used in agriculture, characterizing culture as not intrinsic to a group, but developed through the blended contributions of its members.[5]

The components of culture include personal style, such as how people dress, how they wear their hair, and how they speak. For those that have differing tastes, habits, and experiences, some exercise them and some don't. Through no actions or choice of their own, some people were raised within families where it was commonplace to pursue high levels of academia or even PhDs, while others may have viewed the pursuit of teaching or law enforcement as a major accomplishment. Then there are others that were surrounded by families that were partial toward trade schools or didn't prioritize education at all. Some of your employees were raised in environments that taught them to speak openly and honestly in order to resolve conflict, while others were raised to avoid conflict at all cost and keep their thoughts and perceived problems to themselves.

Ethnic and religious backgrounds may be the source of varied experiences: celebration of holidays, familial closeness or distance, or recreational activities.

Overlaying these differences are values that may come from individuals or may be established by leadership. A company may value rigidly defined roles, secrecy, obedience, and tradition. Or there may be a preference for transparency, open communication, innovation, entrepreneurial spirit, respect, and humility.

We are comfortable within our own culture, where we know the rules and don't have to adapt to unfamiliar behavior. It takes effort to reach beyond our comfort zone to appreciate and embrace the culture of others. But why not experience the richness of another way of interacting with the world?

In many US companies, the culture is uniform, the employees come from similar backgrounds, and the leadership doesn't concern itself with intangibles like customs and attitudes. In this kind of atmosphere, there may be little conflict, but there may also be little opportunity for innovation in response to change in the world. And when a person from a different cultural background enters such a company, she will most likely be misunderstood, looked down on, and blocked from participation in group activities, unless a concerted effort is made to build bridges between the existing culture and the new person's culture. It's no wonder tokenism has been so painful for minorities who are brought in to fulfill a quota and so unsuccessful when it comes to retaining new hires.

The culture of your company should not be stagnant. be a priority to take the time and make the effort to effecti cultures and the wholeness of all of the different people th them. Culture is always evolving, it is unfortunate that fr and within so many work environments, ambiguous c culture have been accepted and cemented by your fou members. These ideals have been perpetually used as a l or prerequisite for being accepted and hired to be a p workforce. Even more importantly, these standards an calls for marginalized people to assimilate is counterprod it comes to reality of the diverse hire's chance at surviv any opportunity to thrive within your organization.

No one group of people should be allowed to shape and cultural norms of a work environment. New hire feel the need to change their personal culture and wh order to fit in.

Culture Breeds Intolerance

It is not until you consciously decide to prioritiz tion of stagnant, exclusive culture that your compa position to make the systemic changes needed to bo eventually abolish disparities. I can assure you that within your company, and all over the world, are hard to be as accommodating and nonthreatening are fully aware that we all have to grow and learn in teams. We need and want to be the best versic at work. The most significant thing I so desperat take from this discussion is this: we should no l

organization, they must be aware of their privilege and be willing to check their biases.

If I didn't believe there were many people like you, who are willing to make this effort, I wouldn't be taking the time to write this book. I know that much of what I've experienced in the workplace is not due to blatant maliciousness. I also know that change could be a matter of life and death for so many of us.

So here I am, baring my soul and expressing my truth. The very least you can do is open your mind and drop any resistance you may be feeling as you consider embracing this work. Vow to try to make life decent for those who spend so much of their lives contributing to the success and growth of your company.

4

A Candid Conversation with a Fellow

Workplace Equity and Inclusion Professional

Kristian Ribberström
Partner and Chief Product Officer
Medici Group

Kristian Ribberström reminded me that it's never too late to learn new things and embrace new practices. Whenever I feel discouraged or as if I don't have what it takes to make a case for equity and inclusion in the workplace, I remember the things that he has taught me.

If you're a corporate leader and hearing the calls for diversifying the country's workforce, you may be thinking, Of course, I'm in favor of fairness for all people, but if we invest money and effort into making these changes, how will my business be affected? I don't want to be railroaded into doing something that is not going to benefit the company overall.

According to Kristian Ribberström of the Medici Group, diversity and inclusion are not only a benefit to employees but give companies a competitive edge. He's not talking about the PR effect that motivates suppliers and clients to work with more diverse companies, although that effect is significant. The Medici Group shows businesses how to use diversity to enhance innovation and responsiveness to our fast-changing world.

As the Medici website points out, "The only constant is change, and our interconnectedness means the world has become far more unpredictable. How can leaders navigate this climate? It takes collaboration, courage, and a new kind of thinking." If your management is dominated by white men who all think more or less alike, innovation is not going to come quickly enough to respond to changes in the outside world. But when the company culture is firmly white-oriented, it's not a simple process to bring diverse talent into a company and create an environment that will enable them to work effectively.

I asked Kristian to talk about the issues he encounters within corporate America and the solutions he implements.

People in Denial

He told me about a recent visit to a well-established company, where he gave a presentation on the positive impact that equity and inclusion have in the workplace. A Black woman, who had a senior position in the firm's marketing department, showed him a picture of several white men in suits. "Here is a photo of our executive leadership team," she said. "As you can see, I will never be part of it."

"Her joke was not only a joke," he told me, "It was one of so many conversations I've had that have helped me develop a strong point of view on representation. If you belong to a minority, and you see that your group is not proportionately represented in media, on boards, in committees, on leadership teams, you will draw conclusions about how accessible such positions are to you." White leaders, said Kristian, do not understand the potent effect of representation. "The white perspective is, the fact that we do not have any Black people in our leadership team does not mean it's harder for them to get a job here. It's just a coincidence. That point of view is absurd."

Although he is not a member of a minority group, Kristian's background has given him the ability to see into the experience of minorities and convey to white people in power how important it is to change that experience. His own initial unwillingness to acknowledge racism also showed him how challenging it is to change attitudes.

Growing up in Sweden, he traveled around Europe extensively with his family. In college, he made a point of studying in other countries and immersing himself in their cultures, and he married a woman from Hungary. In the 1990s, Sweden was flooded with refugees from the US war in Iraq and the civil war in Yugoslavia. Sweden today is a highly diverse country that is also highly segregated.

When a British Jamaican woman, a friend of his wife's, told Kristian that Sweden was racist, he was offended. "No matter how much she tried to explain," he recalls, "I was unable to agree with her, and I became quite defensive. As time went on, I had the opportunity to spend time with people who experienced Sweden in a very different way from myself. I also got to know my wife's friend better and began to see life through her eyes."

Before long, he had an epiphany: "I was the majority." As he saw how much pain racism caused those in the minority, he was horrified with himself and the situation he had been able to ignore. When he shared this insight with other native Swedes, they responded just as defensively as he had.

One of his closest friends was Frans Johannson, who had a Black mother and had grown up in Sweden. Kristian became the sounding board for a book Frans was writing about the powerful effects of bringing together people with different backgrounds. When his book, *The Medici Effect*, was published in 2004 by Harvard Business School Press, it was highly praised by business publications. It has been translated into eighteen languages.

Frans founded the Medici Group with his wife, Sweet Joy Hachuela, and Kristian became their partner in developing a methodology based on Frans' insights. The Medici Group has worked with a slew of top brands, training teams on how diversity and inclusion drive innovation, effectiveness, collaboration, and growth. Kristian is now based in New York City but travels the world giving talks and consultations to companies and governments such as Mastercard, Disney, the European Union, ESPN, and many others.

After giving presentations, he's often approached by Black women who tell him how hard it is to navigate a professional workspace as a woman of color. "They say that people and leaders in the organization often claim that they want to hear about the problems and that they understand. But, in fact, they do not understand, because the situation is much worse than they realize or will admit."

The Benefits of Diversity

When I asked Kristian how he gets beyond that resistance, he reminded me that business leaders all want the same thing: growth and innovation.

If I had any doubt about the importance of having white allies to address racism, my conviction was reinforced by a statement made by a Black woman Kristian once worked with. He told her he sometimes felt inadequate when it came to supporting people of color. Her response was, "You're white. That's your superpower."

Kristian is dedicated to initiating more conversations about inequality and disparity. Even when he's not sure what to say or fears how a situation may make members of a minority group feel, he always remembers that what's most important is his willingness to speak up. Change doesn't happen until those conversations begin.

walked in. "Good morning! How was the commute? Did you have any trouble getting here this morning?" Mindy was a larger woman, not overweight but extremely tall and big-boned, as the old folk would say. She had mid-length, dark hair and a somewhat awkward demeanor.

"Yes, it was such an easy commute. The apartment I found is literally right up the street."

I followed Mindy into the main area of the office.

"That's great...Well, I need to figure out where you'll be sitting. Why don't you take this desk? I don't think anybody's sitting here."

An hour went by, and I was still sitting at the desk waiting for Mindy to return with directives. I decided to go to her office and remind her I was there. She had a puzzled look on her face.

"Oh, Cliff didn't come and grab you? He told me he'd be assisting you with filling out your paperwork."

"No, I haven't seen him."

"Okay, let me see if I can assist you."

Mindy brought me back to the receptionist.

"Connie, do you know where the paperwork is that Cliff mentioned for Talisa to complete?"

"Oh yeah, I have it right here." Connie reached down, grabbed a folder, and handed it to Mindy, who gave it to me.

"When you're done filling these out, take them back to Connie, and she'll put them in the proper place."

5

The CEO Assured Me That He Had My Back

White business leaders typically take the easy route when it comes to dealing with marginalized employees within their workforce. Simply advocating for diversity will never be enough. Inclusive leaders work hard to make the workplace sustainable for all hires once they have joined their organization.

◆

It looked like my big break. I had been handpicked by the CEO of a small yet thriving pharmaceutical event company. The interview was uncomplicated, and the CEO's demeanor was warm and inviting. He insisted on having me call him by his first name, Cliff. He had recently purchased the firm, and while he didn't know a lot about event planning, he seemed to be pretty savvy when it came to running and growing a business.

This was one of the very few times that someone in a position of power actually mentioned having a passion for running a business that placed focus on diversity and inclusion. I thought to myself, *lucky me*. I knew I had the skill set to align with the goals he had for his company, and I hoped to bring him closer to his goal of having a more diverse pool of employees. At the time, the situation truly looked like a win-win.

Cliff informed me that while this company had historically been known for managing pharmaceutical meetings, he anticipated adding incentive trips and events to their service offerings. He felt my experience would allow him to introduce this new sector of business to the company, and to my delight, he hired me on the spot. I knew accepting this offer would be a risk. I would have to move back to Texas, after having lived in San Francisco for the past three years. While it meant that I would have to make sacrifices, I was willing. It wasn't every day that an opportunity to lead incentive trips came around. Incentive trip planners are considered to be the "peerage" of event planning. The planner gets to put together extravagant experiences in luxurious places for the top performers of prestigious organizations. I couldn't believe I had stumbled into such a coveted role. I accepted the offer on the spot and began making plans to move to Texas.

I wasn't offered a relocation package but figured the move would pay for itself with the reduction in the cost of living. I was determined to do a great job at this new company, as one of my closest friends had referred me. I had struggled in the past with office politics, and I was in a period of constantly second-guessing and questioning myself. It was imperative that after making such a sacrifice to move all the way back to Texas that I gave this job my all. It wasn't every day that a friend would help to open a door such as this, and with her reputation on the line, I would go over and beyond to excel at my role. It didn't take long for me to realize that, as in other corporate environments, something within this organization was very, very wrong.

Dismissive Behavior

"Hi, I'm Talisa. Today is my first day. Is Mindy available?"

I'd arrived a few minutes early, dressed in a simple, black, tea-length dress, closed-toe heels, and hair pulled back in a bun. I wore pearl earrings, and my nails were short and neatly manicured with French white tips. Apparently, the woman at the reception desk didn't hear me, although I was standing an arm's length from her, and she certainly saw me as I walked through the door. I couldn't afford to be in a bad mood, so I decided to give her the benefit of the doubt. I repeated myself while projecting my voice a little, now smiling even bigger. "Excuse me, good morning, my name is Talisa, and today is my first day."

"Yeah, Mindy's not here yet. She'll see you and grab you when she walks in."

The receptionist barely looked up at me as she responded. She had a small frame and olive skin, with jet black hair cut into a neat bob with bangs. She was wearing a black and white, horizontal-striped shirt with black slacks and black soft-soled shoes. This was certainly not the most pleasant introduction to the company, but I was feeling optimistic and holding onto the promises made by the new CEO. During the interview, he said he was looking forward to making positive changes as he grew and evolved the business. I saw him as powerful and in charge, the one who called the shots. It felt good knowing that I had a solid connection with him and that he believed in me and my ability to help him have a successful business.

Soon Mindy arrived. I had met her briefly before my interview with the CEO. She seemed genuinely happy to see me as she

It took me twenty minutes to complete all the forms. After going back through each of them to make sure that they were done accurately, I went to return the documents to Connie, as Mindy had instructed me to.

"Hi." I smiled as big as I possibly could without looking like I was joking around. "I finished the documents. Here you go." Again, it appeared that Connie did not hear me. I stepped closer to her desk. "Hey Connie, my documents."

Connie looked up and said, in a condescending tone, "Why are you bringing those to me?"

"Oh, I'm sorry. Mindy told me when I was finished to bring them to you." She rested her fingers under her chin. I pulled the folder back and smiled.

"No worries. Let me just go and talk to Mindy about it."

Confused by Connie's response, Mindy motioned for me to follow her as she walked back out to the reception area. She asked Connie, "Are we not supposed to bring these forms to you?"

"I don't know. I have no idea what I'm supposed to do with them."

"I see. Well, I'll hang onto them and run it by Cliff."

I followed Mindy back toward her office.

"Sorry about that, with the owner being new, some of the processes are kind of wacky. I'll let you know if we need anything else."

"I understand. What should I do now?"

"Ah, good question. Well, just hang out a bit, and I'm sure Cliff will be here soon, and we can figure out the best plan."

"Okay, great, I'll be here."

Keep smiling, keep smiling, keep smiling. Mental gymnastics and repetitive inner dialogue and guidance had become extremely important throughout my career. I returned to my desk with the understanding that Connie had no interest in helping me navigate my new work environment. I could only hope that my day-to-day communication with her would be limited.

Throughout the day, people walked past me saying hello and looking perplexed to see me. I introduced myself to one colleague after another, giving my spiel about how excited I was and how I looked forward to being a part of the team. Most of them were generally pleasant, but no one really took out much time to engage with me. I went to lunch acknowledging the red flags popping up in my mind, but I was determined to remain optimistic. I'd sacrificed a lot to get there, and the promise of true job satisfaction was dangling like a carrot right in front of me. I felt it was up to me to keep myself in good spirits in order to be the best that I could in my new and amazing role.

Opportunities Denied

About three days into this new role, I realized there was no official onboarding process and no one would take the responsibility for training me. I asked several colleagues if I could shadow them or if they would forward me emails that would help me acclimate myself with their processes. I had finally spoken to Cliff, who said that while much of my role would be working on incentive trips and events, that shouldn't stop the rest of the team from training me on the program systems and explaining how their standard events were done within their organization. I came to realize that while Cliff was in power, his hands were somewhat tied because he was so new that he didn't understand the systems or the ins and outs of the business himself. He needed the built-in "brain trust" that came along with the business in order to keep things afloat.

Before long, I found myself at weekly team meetings, where I discovered that event assignments were given out by the salesperson who managed the relationships with the clients. I struggled with being able to determine how he decided who to assign to which client and event. There didn't seem to be any visible pattern, rhyme, or reason. When two weeks had gone by, not only had I not been given an assignment but I still had not been given any proper training. When I asked about the company's intentions for me, or plans for the job I'd been offered, the responses were evasive. At the one-month mark, the situation became alarming. I was asked to assist people who were at lower levels than myself with menial tasks such as ordering candy to fill their gift bags or entering data into spreadsheets. A fair-skinned, less experienced, blue-eyed colleague who was hired the same day I was had been given multiple assignments and was jet setting around the world while I was being told, day after day, to wait.

The Help

Finally, I took my first trip to shadow Mary, a colleague who had been with the firm for four years. Our destination was Florida, where we were going to stay in a beautiful resort on the beach. I arrived at the hotel, then had my first meeting with her in a coffee shop with an eclectic vibe and one of the most stunning views I had ever seen.

The water was so blue as the sunlight reflected off of it. I sat across from Mary, who had long, red hair and freckles. As she explained my responsibilities as an event manager, she spoke to me as if I had never planned an event before. I chose to believe that she wanted to overexplain in an effort to make sure I understood. She described the client we would be working with and explained that she hoped to hand the client over to me. I found her comment both exciting and perplexing—I wasn't supposed to handle any clients in this particular sector of the business, but I was thrilled that there was potential for me to actually own something. Although I was curious about what Mary knew or what plans were being discussed behind the scenes in regard to my role, I refrained from saying anything besides "Okay, great."

We worked all that day and the next, waking up early and going to bed late. I observed Mary's interaction with the client, and all seemed to be going quite well, but on the final day of the meeting, Mary was visibly upset. "What's wrong? Are you okay?" I asked as we packed up our office in preparation for the trip back to Texas.

"I'm so sick of her! Who does she think she is? I told Cliff and Mindy that I am just not the right person to work with this woman. She has the gall to request that I bring her coffee! I'm not going to get her fucking coffee! Who the fuck does she think I am? Pssssh."

I was taken aback by Mary's outburst. I remembered her saying that I would be perfect for this client, despite them being outside the business sector that I was hired for. I also noticed this particular client was a Latina woman, and lastly, I noticed that although clients weren't expected to ask us for things like going to get coffee, I was expected to take on the client simply because Mary didn't want to deal with her. I couldn't believe that Mary had been so bold and insensitive as to blatantly articulate these things to me. I was stunned, hurt, humiliated, and quite frankly, afraid of what the future had in store for me with this company. Even worse, I had to continue to smile and work with Mary while pretending that all was well.

Ridicule

We got through the meeting successfully, and it was time to head home. As we were walking towards the shuttle bus to the airport, Mary looked at me, laughed, and said, "Oh my God, do you think you brought enough luggage?"

I was confused.

"I brought a luggage set to check and a carry-on bag. What do you mean?"

I smiled at her.

"That's just a lot of luggage for four days. Do you always carry that much luggage when you travel? Do you even travel much?" She chuckled under her breath.

"I just wanted to be sure I had everything I needed. It's the first time I've traveled with this company. Better safe than sorry, you know."

I turned away to board the shuttle. My phone went off as the driver grabbed my luggage. I sat down and checked my messages. Mary had sent a group text to all the event planners, including myself. I wasn't surprised, since group texts went out from time to time about the scheduling of work assignments or happenings around the office. What I read was humiliating. I couldn't believe that I was looking at a photo of myself that had been taken from behind.

There I was pulling my luggage and prepping to load the shuttle. The caption read, "Look at this idiot, could she have brought any more luggage? LOL." A colleague had replied, "Oh my God, that's hilarious!" At first I couldn't believe how bold they were to make fun of me in such an egregious way. Once the thread went quiet, it dawned on me. Mary must have accidentally included me in the group text.

I was mortified.

It was hard to go back to work after that incident, but it did serve as concrete validation for my sense of being treated unfairly. Whenever the taunting and bullying in the office led me to question myself—*Was it just me, something I was doing wrong?*—I looked back at that text message. As time went on, the environment became more and more degrading. I went to a therapist so that I could sort out whether I was contributing to the problem at all and what I could do to make life manageable as I attempted to carve out a sustainable space for myself within the office. Week after week, my therapist assured me that I was in the midst of a toxic and inequitable environment with limited options for turning things around to work in my favor.

Racist Remarks

Cliff was clearly enthusiastic about bringing diversity to the recently acquired company. He seemed to think that by hiring me, as an event planner, he could check that goal off his list. After three months of work, I had received no training in the firm's procedures despite my pleas to various colleagues, and I had not been assigned to do what I'd been hired to do, which was to plan and manage full-scale incentive trips and events.

One day, I had a lunch meeting with the company's top sales executive and another event manager. The top sales exec was a white man named Bo. The event manager was a white woman named Riley. In the course of the conversation, Bo shared with us that the firm's previous owners intentionally hired pretty, blonde, blue-eyed girls as planners, as planners. "Hell, it made my job easy. All I had to do was post their head shot on my sales proposal and the clients would eat it up." He laughed.

Feeling humiliated and not sure how to respond, I mimicked his laughter. "Oh, does that explain why I've never been placed on an assignment?"

He looked at me as if I'd just crashed a party and shut it down. With a waning laugh, he turned his attention to cutting his salmon. "Absolutely not," he said. "Of course not. Don't worry, we're working on it."

Social Exclusion

Shortly thereafter I was sent to work at a fast-paced, high-stress event where I was supposed to be getting training from Riley, as she was the assigned event manager. This was also a rare occasion that Bo would go on-site and assist as well. After dealing with a ridiculous level of micromanagement from both of them, we were closing up for the day. I asked Bo, Riley, and a temporary employee if they had dinner plans. They all said they were tired and were going to their rooms to get room service, and with a tone of disapproval Riley reminded me that it probably wouldn't be a good idea, after all, as we had to report to work quite early the next morning. I agreed it had been a long day and said I'd grab room service as well. After getting to my room and reviewing the menu, I decided I'd rather run downstairs and have a quick dinner at the Hard Rock Cafe. It was extremely awkward to walk in and find my three colleagues sitting at a table having drinks. When I said hello, they all looked like they'd seen a ghost. "Hi" and "Hey," they replied, and Bo waved with exaggerated excitement. "So you decided to get out too, huh?"

The women glanced at each other as Bo attempted to pave over the discomfort. I smiled in token Black fashion.

"Yeah, I'm just gonna get an appetizer or something at the bar."

"Well, you're welcome to join us." No doubt his level of seniority and placement on the org chart made him feel that he needed to attempt to cover up that they had purposely avoided having me there.

"Thank you, I don't want to crash your party, and I don't plan to be down here long. Enjoy your meal. I'll see you guys tomorrow."

I walked away with my heart pounding. This incident was more evidence that my future with the company was bleak. My optimism was beginning to fade.

The Double Bind

The following day was hard. The microaggression, micro-management, and condescending statements were at an all-time high. I was demeaned and ignored. Riley told me that I would not be getting any special training from her because she was already over worked, and not being paid enough to do so.

I had been working since five a.m., and it took everything in me to continue trying to insert myself into a team that clearly didn't want me there. In a moment of downtime, Riley, Bo, and a member of the hotel staff huddled in a corner to share small talk, stories, and laughter. I figured this was the perfect time to make my way to our temporary office so that I could charge my phone. There, I discovered a food tray that had been picked over. I realized that lunch had been delivered for the team; needless to say, no one had informed me. I plugged in my phone, picked up a chicken wrap, sat down, and removed my shoes. My feet were killing me. I checked the time and realized that it would be another fifteen minutes before the crowd would be released from the general session to make their way to their next session. I had not been given any specific tasks. I was at the beck and call of anyone I worked with, and much of the time, I was standing around greeting and directing guests looking for things to do. I knew I was always being watched and judged. Not only did I genuinely want to be busy, the last thing I needed was for either of them to say I had been useless during the event. Trying to ask how I could help was proving to work against me, and trying to engage in small talk was hurtful, as they made it clear they had no interest in even pretending I was welcome to join.

The ability to sit in solitude for fifteen minutes with my shoes off, while eating a leftover chicken wrap, was a much-welcomed mental retreat. After about five minutes, I was halfway through my wrap when Riley walked into the office.

She looked at me as though I was the scum on the bottom of her shoe.

I smiled, "How's it going?"

She began slinging boxes around and stacking papers while ignoring my greeting. I put my half-eaten wrap down, got up, put on my shoes, and walked over to her.

"Can I help with anything?"

She slammed a box down and turned toward me.

"What are you doing?"

A bit rattled, I replied. "I'm charging my phone and getting a bite to eat." She sighed as I completed my sentence.

"Is everything ok? Did you need me for something?"

She continued to shuffle papers and ignore me.

"I saw that it was slow, so I took this time to grab a bite. I planned to come back out just before the crowd switches sessions. That happens at one-fifteen, right?"

I was attempting to show her I was fully plugged in and knowledgeable about what was going on.

She started placing items into boxes and replied, "We don't typically eat while events are going on."

"Oh, I'm sorry, I saw the tray here and figured it was okay."

"Yeah, well the temps probably came to grab something and maybe Bo, but I personally don't feel right, as the manager, stopping to eat."

In order to avoid poking the bear any further I asked, "What can I do to help?"

"Don't worry about it!" She rolled her eyes and stormed out of the office. I picked up my phone and followed her. I went back to the registration table where the rest of the staff was posted, and I sat, isolated, while they continued to engage in small talk. Soon after, I noticed Riley eating a bag of pretzels as they chatted to pass the time.

Scapegoated

On the last day of the event, attendees were heading out of the hotel toward the cars our company had arranged to take them to the airport. We had manifests that would tell us when their cars should arrive and when their flights were expected to leave. I volunteered to wish the attendees a safe journey home and offer any assistance as they departed.

It was the perfect refuge. I was able to smile and get smiles back from people that had no hidden agenda or biases toward me. I was simply someone from the event company that cared enough to wish them well as they left.

"Safe travels!" I yelled as attendees piled into the black town cars that were lined up at the curb.

"Excuse me, can you tell me what time my flight leaves?" A tall, white gentleman approached me. He had very deep set brown eyes, sun burnt skin and long, ginger hair pulled up into a messy man bun.

"Sure," I replied as he handed me a piece of paper. "It seems that all you have here is your locator number, correct?" I looked at him with a smile.

He didn't smile back. Visibly frustrated he replied, "I don't know. I just know I need to get out of here." I wasn't at all fazed by his frustration. I genuinely wanted to help. "Do you mind if I take this piece of paper to one of my colleagues? They can assist us with finding out more info." He looked reluctant to agree but he had no obvious alternative. I took the document to Bo, who was still hanging out in the lobby of the hotel, chatting with Riley and the clients who had hosted the event. I pulled him aside to tell him the guest was upset and wanted to know when his flight would be leaving. After digging around our database, we discovered the gentleman had in fact missed his flight. "So how do we handle this?" I asked.

"Let me go and talk to him," Bo said dismissively. I followed him as I wanted to make sure he knew which man was having the issue, and I was curious to see how he would handle it.

The man was on the phone, pacing back and forth, loose pieces of his long hair blowing in the wind. I waved to get his attention. "Hello there, this is my colleague, and he may be able to help you." The man abruptly ended his phone call.

"Hi sir, it seems your flight left at about noon." Bo attempted to explain his findings, when the man interrupted him.

"What the fuck?! This shouldn't have happened. I need to get to another meeting." The expression on Bo's face was one of someone who had been slapped.

"Sir, if you want to come back inside with me, we can help you book another flight."

"I'm not doing shit! This shouldn't have happened, and she shouldn't be allowed to make these kinds of fuck-ups!" The man yelled as he pointed at me.

It was my third day of torture and confusion. I'd worked from sunup to sundown, only to be abused, and now a guest was blaming me for his missed flight. All I could think to myself was, I would surely be getting the can now. In a panic I replied, "I'm sorry sir. What did I do?"

"You're just standing there with a shit-eating grin on your little face, and I've got places I need to be."

He looked at Bo for approval.

"This is really ridiculous. She should have put me in a car to get me to my flight."

I nervously replied, "I am so sorry, sir, there was nothing I could do. I just wanted to help, so I went to find a manager. I am so, so sorry."

Bo interrupted me by putting his hand up in my face. "Just stop! Sir, please come this way, and we'll get this taken care of."

I ran into the nearest bathroom and locked myself in a stall to bawl my eyes out. There was no resolving this. I'd done nothing wrong, and here I was being hung out to dry.

When it was time for us to pack up our office and leave, Bo and Riley continued to ignore me as they conversed. Bo told Riley about the experience with the angry man. "He was such a dick. Like, dude, no one can be held responsible for your missed flight."

I thought to myself, finally some vindication. Against my better judgment, I decided this might be a safe place to insert myself into the conversation.

"I couldn't believe he was blaming me."

Bo replied, "Well, you should have just said nothing. You only made things worse."

The invasive knot in my stomach grew larger.

"What do you mean? I apologized."

"I was there, I was telling him I would take care of it. You didn't need to insert yourself."

I took a deep gulp of what had to be my pride.

"I apologized because he said it was my fault, I didn't realize an apology would be looked at as a bad thing. I'm sorry...I think...I hope that's okay. I'm sorry."

No one responded.

I traveled back to town knowing that I would have to finally make Cliff aware that things were not going well.

The Result of Calling Out Discrimination

Cliff agreed to have lunch with me the following week. At our meeting, I reiterated how much I had sacrificed to move to Texas to take the job and how excited I was to be a part of the team. I gave him specific examples of how I was not being trained and how I'd been blatantly told by people tasked to train me that they wouldn't. I told him many coworkers had been vocal about their disapproval of my taking on incentive events without any of them having been asked to do so.

I told him about the sales manager mentioning the ease of pitching women with blonde hair and blue eyes to clients. I explained how it felt to be told I should be the one to cater to a Latina woman who requests that coffee be brought to her during meetings and events.

I showed him that embarrassing group text message, where I was the brunt of a joke, along with examples of condescending emails, my ignored attempts to engage and participate, and my efforts to be accommodating in situations that were unbearable. He looked me in the eyes and assured me that he was not surprised to hear anything I was sharing. He was so passionate in his response that I described it to my therapist as a declaration that he made, stating that this particular behavior was not the kind of behavior he envisioned happening at his company, and that he simply would not tolerate it. He confided in me that the company had previous issues with racism prior to him taking over, and that he was very happy to have me and appreciated my patience as he worked to shift the dynamics.

"I truly regret that this happened. You should have come to me sooner." He assured me things would change, and I'd have the opportunity to finally do the job I was hired to do.

I never saw Cliff again after that meeting.

A few days later I received an email from Kathy, a representative from a third-party human resources firm. Kathy was reaching out to follow up on my conversation with Cliff. She scheduled a face-to-face meeting with me to discuss my experiences with the company.

I was plagued with anxiety as I waited for two days to meet with her. I had no work assignments, and everyone was avoiding me. The days dragged, and my anxiety became more and more debilitating. Finally, the day of the meeting arrived. Kathy was an older, white woman with a strawberry blonde pixie haircut. She wore a floral dress and a denim jacket. I greeted her with a smile, in return I was met with a hollow expression.

I repeated to her the stories I had shared with Cliff a few days before. She appeared to be carefully taking notes while maintaining a poker face. It took me an hour to get through all my documentation. Again, I emphasized my enthusiasm and hopes for the job.

"Well, thank you for sharing, Talisa. I will take this information and conduct an investigation. Once I've gathered my information and done my due diligence, I will circle back to you with our plan for next steps. Do you have any questions?" There was a long pause.

"No, I don't. Thank you for taking the time to hear me out today."

I didn't know what else to say. I wasn't even sure how to feel. I hadn't heard from Cliff since our meeting. I started to doubt that he would keep his promise to protect me. I was at Kathy's mercy. The only thing I could do now was wait.

For three long days, Kathy called meetings with everyone in the office, one after the other. I saw the looks of discomfort on their faces as they walked in and out of the room. I heard the whispers as they gathered in the break room. I struggled to get responses from anyone in regard to any actual work that I could do. I decided to send an email to Cliff letting him know that I'd spoken with Kathy, and that since my meeting with him, I was still struggling to find a way to insert myself and contribute. I never got a reply from him.

I discussed my situation with friends and my therapist. When they suggested my job was in jeopardy, I referred to my recent conversation with Cliff. His reassurance was all I had as I attempted to calm my angst. I convinced myself that there was no way he would allow anything bad to happen to me; in fact, at the end of this "investigation," he would have enough inside information to finally begin creating the more inclusive environment we had discussed.

I trusted Kathy would work to ensure that I was given proper training and an opportunity to do the job I was hired to do. I had been completely transparent and honest, provided lots of supporting documentation and I'd shown them how I had remained both pleasant and accommodating while attempting to navigate the situation on my own.

Finally, she asked to meet with me again to discuss her findings. I entered the room and began to shiver, both because of the temperature and because of my overwhelming nervousness.

"So, we've completed our investigation and have concluded that you're not a good fit for our organization."

My heart dropped. I couldn't believe what I was hearing.

"No one here can corroborate your experience."

With my voice trembling, I asked, "What do you mean?" She looked annoyed by my question.

"Everyone here agrees you have been trained, but you're simply not able to do the job."

"But I've never been able to do the job. I don't even have all the necessary logins to the software, so how is it possible that I've been trained?"

Kathy let out a long sigh.

"There's really no need for you to try to defend yourself. You would never be happy here, anyway. No one agrees with your perception of things."

"Of course they don't. I'm not part of the in-crowd. I'm not their friend."

Kathy looked as though she couldn't be bothered.

"So why would you even want to work here if that's the case? Why not go somewhere that you can actually be friends with people?"

Taken aback by this statement, I stammered, "Cliff promised me he wouldn't let this happen. He assured me the company hadn't been very inclusive in the past, and he would make sure I was given the same opportunities as everyone else."

"Talisa, you even have issues with clients."

"What?! I've never been assigned a client. My interaction or communication has been extremely minimal with any clients."

I could barely get my words out. Kathy rolled her eyes.

"You didn't cause a client to miss his flight?"

"Oh my God! What?! No!"

Kathy stopped me before I could explain further.

"I have a box here for you to pack up your belongings, and we will mail your last check to you within seventy-two hours."

I got up from my seat, packed up my belongings, and escorted myself out of the office.

6

A Candid Conversation
with a White Racial Equity Activist

Colin Stokes
Director of Communications, Outreach, and
Engagement Metropolitan Council for Educational
Opportunity Boston, MA

When I think of Colin Stokes, I am reminded of the phrase, "each one, teach one." Colin Stokes is the epitome of an ally dedicated to the movement of dismantling racism. With passion and a genuine desire to be and do better, Colin has dedicated his life to this work while sharing his insights and solutions with others.

◆

Perhaps you have begun to embrace the importance of diversity and inclusion within your company, but you're wondering how you and your company will fit into this new paradigm that I am proposing. You may not think of yourself as a racist, but you might have to make shifts in thought and behavior to make such a radical change in your business. Will these shifts be hard or easy to make? Will your own life be changed for the better?

You might be interested to hear how Colin Stokes dealt with his discovery of unconscious bias within himself. In his TEDx talks, he explains how he came to recognize the racial disparities in his workplace and resolved to change both himself and the environment he worked in.

In his fifteen years of working for nonprofits that are focused on K-12 education, Colin has witnessed the inequities that minorities encounter, not only in the way students are treated but also in how organizations hire, promote, and make decisions that favor white people. In fact, early in his career, he feels he unintentionally made those disparities worse.

"I wasn't resistant to change," he explained, "but I was naive. I was the white liberal that Martin Luther King, Jr, warned against. I assumed the arc of justice was bending along as intended; I believed that being nice was a kind of magic spell that made me immune to criticism. I changed all too slowly, as I worked alongside more people of color who were honest with me. Social media also allowed me to learn directly from writers of color without breaking the white code of silence."

White Privilege

Growing up nonathletic and Jewish in San Antonio, Colin learned early on what exclusion felt like. He sympathized with those on the outside rather than those in power. But he was also white, male, and straight. "I was showered with the benefits that came with those characteristics," he said, "and with the propaganda that those benefits were earned."

He attended Harvard, as his father had, found work as an actor in New York City, and married his white college girlfriend. After the birth of their first child, the couple sold the fixer-upper Manhattan apartment their parents had helped them buy, and they moved in with his wife's parents rent-free in an expensive Boston suburb. "I thought of this 'luck' as within a normal scope of random good fortune. It was the American Dream!"

Now that Colin had a family, it was time to find a more consistent job. He wanted to do something that made him feel good, so he followed his social networks to a role in the central office of an education nonprofit. The leadership and upper management were almost all white graduates of elite schools. Some of the field staff, who worked with children and were paid much less than the managers, were Black or Latinx, and a number of the entry-level and administrative staff were too.

"I noticed but didn't reflect on these patterns," Colin recalled. "I didn't even realize race was a component of the organization's mission, maybe because it was coded as 'urban' and 'diverse' and 'socioeconomically disadvantaged.' I cringe now at the damage I did then."

In his work in marketing and fundraising, Colin routinely framed traumatic parts of people's lives in broad, stereotypical tropes in order to coax bigger donations from the organization's wealthy white sponsors. Meanwhile, when white and Latinx colleagues asked him for mentoring in his skill set, he didn't hesitate. But when Black men and women tried to build these professional relationships, he met with them perfunctorily and did not follow through. "This hurts me most to remember, because I directly deprived people of opportunity."

Awakening to Inequality

But gradually he started to see what had been invisible to him. Working alongside people with different norms—the language, gestures, and style of dress of contemporary Black culture—it dawned on him that he didn't live in America; he lived in White America. And whether or not he had been justified in feeling excluded in Texas or at Harvard, he realized that in the greater society, he was "in the club."

"The club gave me great opportunities, and I tried to make them count," he said. "I was invited to give a local TED talk because of my theater background, and I spoke about the representation of boys and girls in children's movies. It was very well received and made me feel like a good feminist. But a Black male colleague named Brian, after praising the talk, asked me why I hadn't talked about the representation of different races in popular culture. I didn't have an answer. I felt like race was an area I had no right to speak about or any knowledge of. But his question made me realize I had not felt any curiosity about it either."

That winter, in 2012, Trayvon Martin, a seventeen-year-old African American boy, was fatally shot by George Zimmerman, the neighborhood watch coordinator for the gated community where Martin was visiting relatives at the time of the shooting. Outrage over the killing sparked the start of the Black Lives Matter movement. "My workplace, or at least part of it, was reeling," Colin said. "I noticed that the levels of my coworkers' despair differed by color. It was time to learn more. I added Black publications to my Facebook feed and got a daily master class in the rage, grief, determination, and humanity of Black Americans. I was slowly replacing the shockingly misleading white narrative with a truer one. It was creating the soil for a new sense of myself to grow."

He tried to apply his new insights to his work at the nonprofit, looking critically at his own work and embracing feedback from colleagues of color, while also examining the organization itself. He noticed that people who spoke up about interpersonal or structural biases were ignored, frowned on, or driven out. "I didn't take any bold actions to fight this pattern beyond sympathy, unfortunately. But eventually I quit. I was hungry for spaces where honesty around racism was not assumed to be dangerous and where I could learn from those brave enough to teach."

Since then, he's taken classes, read books, watched films, and gradually formed new friendships outside of the white bubble. These experiences have helped him rethink his story. "I see that I have lived a segregated life. The segregation was designed to benefit me, not deprive me; but in a spiritual way, it has deprived me. It has poisoned me with bias, inhibited my compassion, and blocked me from being part of the full human community."

Learning and Teaching

Now his greatest fulfillment comes from bringing others along the path he has taken. Through talks, workshops, writing, neighborhood activism, or just the Black Lives Matter sign by his mailbox in that rich Boston suburb, he's trying to shake more white people awake. He found a new job at METCO, a nonprofit that was created by African Americans in partnership with white suburbanites to integrate public schools.

"At the very least, I can create ways for diverse groups of people to come to a deeper understanding of each other and the history of American racism we have inherited. But I'm also striving to unleash the power society gives me to make transformative change. When a person who has been granted full access to the inside starts to fight for inclusion and justice, maybe he can do more than open doors. Maybe he can tear down some walls.

"The vast majority of individuals who are standing in the way of a fair world are white men. Yet I find myself frequently the only white man at an event or workshop focused on racial justice. This is crazy. I figure the more of us that are visible, saying true things and trying to work toward the world we need, the more of us will see this is a viable, even infinitely richer, path to take."

7

Will I Ever Be Good Enough?

I drove a BMW and had a closet full of designer bags and shoes. And of course, I had a company laptop and credit card. Things looked good from the outside. No one would have dreamed of the hell I was going through while being a Black woman working in corporate America.

"**A**re you ok? That was hard to watch." Ami rubbed my arm as I pressed my back against the bathroom door. The last thing I needed was for another coworker to discover that I was hiding out in there, weeping.

"I'm not." I said between sniffles.

"I'm so sorry, I can't believe she did that."

"Have you seen her treat anyone else like this before?" I lifted my head, filled with shame and with eyes welled.

"I haven't. She's been moody lately, but that was a bit extreme. I know it took everything in you to sit there and take it."

This moment felt surreal. Here I was in my thirties, in a bathroom crying because I had been hit and cursed out at work.

I know what you're thinking, There is no way. Well, you're wrong. It happened, and at the time I felt like I had to take it. I was fairly new on the job, and the the owner was a Trump supporting, narcissistic, demented, elderly, white woman. Her mental decline was constantly discussed around the office. Management, which was her daughter and two sons, dared not challenge her and advise her to retire.

Brandy had been asked to train me on how to type and send company emails. I can imagine that once again you're questioning the authenticity of my statement. Well, once again, I'm telling you that it's the truth. I had far more experience than young, white Brandy. She stood about five-foot-four, with mid-length, strawberry blonde hair. She was about six months pregnant with her first child. It didn't take me very long to realize that Brandy and everyone else in the office was riddled with anxiety and always felt like they were on the verge of losing their jobs. The turnover was ridiculously high, and everything from the Glassdoor reviews to the unprofessional interview told me that I was walking into a lion's den. Now, I'm sure you're wondering why I would even apply or accept the role. The simple answer is, I needed it, at least I felt like I did at that time.

Slapped!

The owner was a tyrant. Her requirements for us were inconceivable. Brandy had been asked to sit behind me and watch me answer emails. She was instructed to tell me the exact words to type and how to go about filing and deleting them as they entered my inbox throughout the day.

"Dear James comma, now hit space, hit space again. HIT IT AGAIN!" My hands shook as she yelled out her demands.

"Now go to the other screen and copy the exact text I sent you and place it below the greeting."

I began to copy the text.

"How many times do I have to tell you that you have to use the shortcut?"

"Pardon me?" I was genuinely confused. I had copied the text and placed it on the line below the greeting exactly as she had asked me to.

"I TOLD YOU THAT IS NOT THE WAY WE COPY AND PASTE HERE! CHECK YOUR EMAIL AGAIN! I SENT YOU THE SHORTCUTS!"

My hands shook as I went back through the emails she had flooded my inbox with earlier that morning. She let out a sigh so loud that I could feel her warm breath on the back of my neck.

"Let me do it!" She said as she reached over me and began sorting through my emails. "If you would file the e-mails away like I told you to, we wouldn't have to go digging through all of these, and maybe you would have had time to actually read them before I got here." Her spit droplets hit the side of my face; I was afraid to wipe them away as she stared at me in disapproval.

Everything about this moment took me back to childhood. This person was in control, and it was up to me to find a way to keep her from exploding. Her behavior was clearly irrational, but I didn't have the latitude to defend myself. "Got it? Can you hear?" With my head held down, I nodded to show that I'd heard her. She deleted the entire email draft. "Now, let's try this again."

With my heart racing, I noticed the other three white women and another colleague, a woman of color from the Virgin Islands had all heard me being berated. Now my anxiety was accompanied by sheer humiliation. I started over by typing Dear James comma. Under normal circumstances, I could have typed a professional email in two seconds flat with my eyes closed, but at this moment I was physically and mentally struggling and completely overwhelmed. I hit the return bar and stalled. As I sat there replaying her directives in my head, I felt a sting on my hand.

"Hit space two times! How hard is that to accomplish?"

My reflexes caused me to jump and my head collided with her shoulder. "Jesus Christ! Do you even want to be here?!" I sat frozen, unable to answer as she had already shown me that any response would be dismissed or potentially used against me. "NOW USE THE STEPS THAT WE GAVE YOU! THAT'S HOW SHE SAID YOU NEEDED TO DO IT, NOT THE WAY THAT YOU HAVE BEEN!" She was leaning over me yelling, and by now everyone in the office had become curious and unapologetic voyeurs. With my head hung low, I took a deep breath and prepared to try again. "Just stop!" She sighed. "I need to go to a meeting. We can try this again after lunch."

She strode off, and I waited until she was out of sight to make my dash to the ladies' room.

Damned If I Did, Damned If I Didn't

My last day with this company was especially ironic. After months of abuse, I was scheduled to manage an event that I was actually looking forward to. Most of our assignments required travel, and this was a rare occasion for me to work on a local event and stay in a cool boutique hotel that wasn't far from where I lived.. The client, Whitney, was a joy to work with.

"You're so amazing Talisa," she told me as we ended our meeting. "You've thought of absolutely everything. I have to have you work with us moving forward. Thank you so much."

Hearing compliments from my clients meant more to me than they could have ever imagined. It was the one thing I could depend on to help me gauge and determine reality versus gaslighting. I loved being a resource for my clients and making their lives easier.

We were both shocked to see Pam, the owner of my company, and Stacey, my director, walk into the hotel lobby. She believed them when they said they just wanted to drop by and introduce themselves, but I knew they were there to spy on me. I greeted them, pretending their presence was perfectly normal and expected.

Per usual, Pam's shoulders were covered in dandruff, and the back of her pants were stained. A few weeks earlier she had asked me to make a purchase for an upcoming event. Within days she had forgotten her directive, accused me of making a major error, and made a scene about how much I had cost the company. I struggled with whether to save myself or not. In conversations with colleagues, I weighed the options and was advised by an influential, long-standing member of management that I should prove to her that she had requested the purchase. This controversy was such a pressing issue around the office that we referred to it as *PurchaseGate*.

After introducing Pam to the client, Pam immediately asked, "So, how are things going?"

"Oh my God, I can't say enough about how wonderful things have been." Pam and Stacey glanced at each other. Pam shook her head. "Everyone is so happy, the transportation went smoothly, the hotel is lovely, the food is delicious, and Talisa keeps my glass full of Diet Dr. Pepper. What more could I ask for?"

"Well it's great to hear that. We always enjoy working with you all. We have managed your meetings for going on ten years now," Pam said.

"Yes, our president told me I'd have no worries when working with you. Oh, I hate to run ladies, but I have to go and make an important phone call. Did you need anything from me?"

"Oh no, go right ahead. Enjoy the rest of your time here."

As Whitney sprinted away, I offered to show them around. As awkward as the situation was, I maintained my professionalism and further confirmed that I had things under control. I would spend another two nights there getting this client and all of the attendees through a series of meetings and events.

The day I returned to the office, Pam was out. She rarely missed a day of work. Stacey was extremely short with me and seemed to be too busy to engage until she asked me to come to her office. She looked as though someone had stolen her puppy.

Stacey had been a witness to much of what I had gone through and had become my secret ally. She sympathized with me when I was treated unfairly and applauded my successes, but aside from asking Brandy to apologize to me for the copy-and-paste fiasco, she was never bold enough to support me outside her closed office door.

She and the other witnesses to PurchaseGate could vouch for the fact that I had simply followed Pam's instructions, but they refused to do so in any capacity that might serve as my redemption. Stacey even went so far as to admit that PurchaseGate was the moment she had to back off and distance herself from me. She warned me there was an X on my back, and she didn't want her perceived affinity towards me to create issues for her.

I took a seat at her desk and took a deep breath of the lavender-scented aromatherapy oil that filled her office.

"I want to commend you on your professionalism with Whitney and the event you just wrapped up. I was blown away by how you greeted us, introduced us, and even showed us around. That says a lot about you."

"Thank you, but of course, my professionalism is a reflection of my work ethic and and reputation. I wouldn't do anything to jeopardize that."

I hated the fact that there was such a low expectation when it came to my ability to be professional, whether under pressure or not.

"I know."

She let out a huge sigh and looked down at the floor.

"I'm sorry. She told me to let you go."

Although I wasn't surprised, my heart still dropped. I felt horrible, but I also felt a sense of relief. It seemed there was nothing that they could do to me that would have caused me to walk away. Some part of me welcomed the push out of the door.

"Did she say why?"

"It was the purchase."

I got up from my seat and said goodbye. I glanced back to look at Stacey one more time.

She was wiping a tear from her eye.

8

A Bitter Confession

White women in America have a history of using their racial privilege as a weapon against minorities. Many of these women feel entitled to sabotage the lives and livelihoods of those who are different from them. They employ manipulative and strategically orchestrated behaviors, such as hysterically crying and shaking in order to garner sympathy from onlookers. Business leaders must begin to acknowledge the havoc that these women create within their organizations and in the lives of their colleagues.

◆

To the countless white women that I have encountered in my career—some in leadership roles, others who have reported to me, and most who have worked alongside me—this is my confession to you.

I heard you when you said, "I'm sick of feeling pressured to agree that minorities deserve special treatment and sensitivity because of things that happened years ago. We all have problems."

I'm in no way denying that we all have problems, but I'm asking you to stop denying that all of these years later we have yet to reach a real space of equality. It will take people like you stepping outside of your own reality to examine yourself and to take time to truly reflect, in order to admit that you inherently have it better than others.

I've also heard you speak of how tired you are of being made to feel guilty about something that you had absolutely nothing to do with, events that happened generations before you were born. You've said this to me even though I've never mentioned anything about race or inequality to you. It's as if you needed to let me know in advance that you would not be taking any responsibility for anything I might perceive as racist or unfair.

When I found myself in situations where you exercised your white privilege or aided in creating an environment that was detrimental to my well-being, I reluctantly spoke up. You responded with one of your most trusted tools: tone policing. This move took the focus off the transgression against my rights and dignity, changing my attempt to make a valid case into a threat to your white fragility. Your hurt, outrage, and tears demonstrated your rejection of the idea that whiteness in America is privileged and normalized in virtually every social and institutional structure. You and the rest of our white colleagues escaped accountability while reinforcing the very privilege that I attempted to call out. Your feelings and your perception were prioritized above any potential damage that had been done to me; your claim that I've made you uncomfortable landed me back in the unemployment line, with no questions asked.

For years you have taunted me. In addition to having to walk on eggshells in order to get what I needed to properly do my job, I've had to try to make it appear that I was not aware of or bothered by your arrogance. We both know you were not required to be half as good as me, yet I had to struggle to pretend this wasn't the case in order to avoid making you feel judged.

I've tried time and time again to be your friend. You've made it practically impossible, as you spoke openly about how you hate when Black people "play the race card." You've discussed how you feel uncomfortable around certain employees and clients because you have nothing in common with them.

I imagine I sound, in this letter, like the typical "angry Black woman." I'm hesitant to offer a disclaimer, as I'm exhausted with the idea of having to explain myself; however, I want to present myself and my case in the most transparent way possible. I want to assure you that this message isn't meant to be abrasive, but the fact of the matter is, it comes from a place of real pain and suffering.

Most of you were raised to experience your racially-based advantages as fair and normal. I'm here to tell you they're not, except when considered from inside the bubble that insulates you from the real world. If you are reading this book, it is my hope that you are in a place where you are ready to step outside of yourself and open your mind to the possibility that you have contributed to white supremacy and racial injustice, while believing in superficial racial tolerance.

You've utilized your unacknowledged power to isolate and ultimately expel me. You probably convinced yourself that I deserved it for being incompetent, ghetto, country, or rude. It's even easier for you to live with yourself when your white counterparts back you up, despite your lack of evidence or substantiated reasons for having a problem with me.

It's simple for you to get the corroboration of your white counterparts. After all, each of you has mastered the act of tuning me out when I defend myself. In fact, you find a way to let me know in advance that if I attempt to do so, I'll be labeled "defensive," which equates to "unprofessional" and unworthy of being a part of your team. My fortune within corporate America has always been held hostage by white solidarity.

You treat me differently. When you discuss me with your family and friends, you refer to me as "the Black girl at work." I make you uncomfortable, especially when I speak with intelligence, in which case you say I'm being condescending. If I relax, you think I'm being overly familiar. If I can't figure out the coded language you speak in, you consider me inauthentic and a waste of your time.

You are applauded when you speak up in meetings and go against the grain, while I am viewed as aggressive and hard to deal with. You are viewed as shy or quiet when you opt to fly under the radar, while I am viewed as antisocial and inept.

My very existence makes you angry, and when just one of you has had enough, you systematically come together to create a plan to make me as uncomfortable as possible. The experience that hurts the most is when you see and quietly acknowledge the disparities, yet you fail to say anything in my defense when it truly matters.

I understand that my livelihood and personal goals are not at the top of your list of priorities. I'm not saying they have to be. I am, however, calling out harsh truths that I can only hope will begin to change over time. If you can't speak up, at the very least make a vow to remove yourself from the process that causes harm.

My differences and uniqueness are no threat to you. My choice to speak up or lay low has more to do with my internal fears than they have to do with you. The guilt that you feel because it's obvious that I have to work ten times harder than you just to be considered average shouldn't be a reason for you to be so cavalier while secretly harboring a strong desire for me to go away. And let me assure you that I am not looking for your sympathy or any special handouts. I simply want the same opportunities that you have: to do my work without being micromanaged, taunted, and harassed.

You've yelled at me, called me an idiot, refused to train me, physically assaulted me, taken credit for my work, and blatantly lied about me. As a result, I was reprimanded or fired for bringing your behavior to the attention of those in authority. The facts never mattered. My skin color made me wrong, and you never had to take any responsibility for your deceitful actions.

My Proposal for Atonement and Reconciliation

If there is anything in you that cares, I'd like to offer you a few steps toward being a person who no longer contributes to the sabotage of innocent people. First, you have to acknowledge your privilege. I have come to realize that it is exceedingly difficult for many white people to make this admission, so if you find yourself resisting, please understand that most people do. I challenge you to move beyond the resistance and have an open mind that allows you to see beyond yourself and your subconscious beliefs.

I challenge you to address your fears and anxieties about being in relationships with people that don't look, act, and speak like you. Begin with your social life. Find ways to ease into situations where you will find yourself truly getting to know people that you typically wouldn't gravitate toward. You will be surprised to find out how much you actually have in common. You will discover that in many cases, it is perfectly okay to engage in conversations about racism, and how you can become anti-racist. Your willingness to have an open and honest discussion will most likely be welcomed.

Lastly, accept the fact that many of us encounter and deal with racism on a day-to-day basis. Bullying us into silence and attempting to shame us for speaking about mistreatment is counterproductive to the growth of our society and our workplaces. In fact, bringing those instances of abuse to light is necessary if we are going to understand each other. I believe that if we work at it despite the discomfort that may arise, we can begin to make peace.

9

Always On the Defense

So many times, there was simply no way out of the preposterous scenarios that my white colleagues placed me in. When standing at a crossroads, I knew they would manage to find a way to ensure that both roads lead to a dead end.

◆

Hi Jay,

As you can see in the email I've attached, on June 3, 2018, we made an agreement that the cost for breakfast would be $78 per person with a guaranteed minimum of 700 guests. You can also see in the same email, I mentioned that 50% of the audience would be vegan or vegetarian. I'm not sure where the confusion came in, but we are down to the wire, and half of the attendees will be expecting meals that accommodate their special requests.

Please let me know how I can help to make sure that we are able to deliver this under such tight time constraints. I'm willing to throw on an apron and work in the kitchen if you find yourself needing to send staff out, and I'm sure I can find others from my team to do the same.

I look forward to hearing back from you.

Thanks,
Tali

I frantically selected high priority and hit *send*, with my (white) colleagues, Ellie and Janet, cc'd. Here I was again, in fight-or-flight mode, presenting documentation in an effort to defend myself because I was being positioned as a scapegoat.

I had been in contact with Jay, the caterer, for weeks as we planned the detailed menus for a major event. Everything went fine until the day before the conference, when Jay informed Ellie and me that he didn't have enough vegan meals prepared to meet our requirements. He became defensive, insisting I had never mentioned the need for the vegan meals.

"I'm sorry for the confusion," I replied, "but we have the requirements listed on all of the contracts and in several places throughout our email communication."

"You show me where I agreed to that!" He began to shout.

"Just don't," Ellie said to me, raising her hand to shut me down.

They continued to go back and forth as if I wasn't there.

Powerless, the only thing I could do was send the email and documentation that proved I wasn't the culprit in this situation. I knew the documentation wouldn't help me, but at least deep down inside, everyone would be aware that this situation wasn't my fault.

Ellie had a talk with me about how hard the job was and how she understood if I felt frustrated. She acknowledged, in a roundabout way, that Jay was not taking responsibility for dropping the ball but informed me that she and Janet had come up with a solution to make things work. She told me that in order to be good at my job and make it with the company, I would have to go and apologize to him. She believed I shouldn't have sent the email and needed to learn not to be so defensive. I asked her for specific examples of times that I had been defensive, and she did her dismissive hand-up gesture again. "Listen, just go and say you're sorry and that you're looking forward to having a great time pleasing the clients over the next few days."

While I didn't apologize to Jay, I did greet him with a huge smile and spoke with him the rest of the day as if the blowup had never occurred. I complimented him on his presentation and the flavor of the foods. I convinced myself that the conflict was water under the bridge. I had to. There was no other way to get through the day.

The next morning, one of the members of the client team approached me as attendees were grabbing their breakfast. "Hey Tali, I don't see an option for a vegan meal here on the buffet."

"Oh no! Let me check on that for you."

My heart raced. Despite my asking, Ellie hadn't told me how they'd decided to handle the vegan issue.

When I found her, she said, "I ordered the clients some more food, all vegan. I need you to go and pick it up and work with Jay to set up a special space for them to go and grab it."

I did as instructed, and Jay was not happy.

"Why am I having to do this?"

He confronted me with obvious frustration.

"I'm really sorry, this is per Ellie's instructions, and I'm happy to set it all up if you tell me where to do it."

He rolled his eyes.

"You know, I'm not obligated to do any of this. I've been catering for twenty-five years, and I've never seen people act like this. Our food options are fine."

"Yeah, I hear you."

I didn't dare say much. I wasn't sure how my words could be twisted and used against me. I also wanted to show solidarity with Jay to keep him from trying to sabotage me again.

I'm Not at Liberty to Speak the Way You Do

"Hey, would you please start pushing the crowd out of here and into the auditorium? We're about to get started." A tall, slender, mature white woman in a suit startled me.

"Oh, do we have a bell?" I asked. "Or maybe a wine glass and fork?"

"No, just push them. Get your temp staff to push them and just yell."

She appeared extremely hasty and impatient.

I soon realized this woman was a contractor who had a long-standing relationship with our company. She was helping manage the timeline of the main event for the audio-visual department. I immediately directed several members of the temp staff to ask attendees to please start making their way into the auditorium.

The slender woman was yelling while waving her arms in the air, "Everyone, head this way to the auditorium! We've got a show to start!"

I walked around, smiling and informing individuals and small clusters of people that the event would soon be starting. At one moment, I caught the woman's eye as she was herding the crowd, and I was sure that she was purposely giving me a nasty look. I told myself that I was overreacting. She was probably stressed out, and her facial expression had nothing to do with me.

As the final few stragglers found their way to the auditorium, Ellie appeared. Before I could greet her, I felt someone yank me by the arm. "Hey there, not sure how much you know about managing events, but when I say move the crowd, you have to move the fucking crowd!"

I was right, the tall woman was annoyed and had, in fact, intended to give me that threatening look of displeasure.

"I did, I've been here the whole time moving the crowd."

Ellie was now between us. "Wait, what's going on?"

"You know how it is when the crowd won't move. You've gotta herd 'em like cows."

I rushed to defend myself.

"I did, I walked around, and I told everyone that we were starting soon."

Ellie shushed me as usual.

"When you have to move this amount of people," said the woman, "you don't tell them individually. I have to keep my timeline tight." She walked away.

"Ellie, I told the people to move, and I gathered members of the temp team to help. I'm not sure what the problem is, everyone was seated on time."

"Yeah, well you heard what she said. She knows this stuff. Just try listening and learning. Again, not everything has to be defended."

I knew my strategy for moving the crowd had been effective. I also knew how people would have reacted to a Black woman yelling at them while waving her arms in the air and behaving as aggressively as the tall, slender white woman.

Gaslighting

On the final day of the conference, Jay and I were breaking down the special food station, which it turned out none of the clients had even used. Jay took advantage of our solitude and dumped a pretty vehement rant on me.

"I'm done dealing with those bitches you work with," he said. "If I'd known I was going to have to do this shit, I wouldn't have agreed to work with your company."

After three days of tiptoeing around Jay and trying to appease him, I now had to listen to him vent about the irrational clients, our unprofessional company, and that "bitch" Ellie. Being on the receiving end of his anger made me feel like it was actually directed at me.

Shortly after, Ellie and Janet could see that I was visibly upset. I described the conversation to them, as well as the series of microaggressions from Jay over the past three days. "He's been all right towards me," said Ellie, and Janet dismissed my complaints completely.

But Ellie wanted to see how Jay would behave in a meeting with the three of us. Where would he place the blame for his frustration? She set up a debriefing for the following morning without warning him that Janet and I would be present. Meanwhile, Janet gave me a demeaning lecture on how to communicate tactfully with vendors.

"I'm sorry," I said, "but this is not a matter of me needing to change anything. This is a very unprofessional and rude man who has given me hell over the past few days."

Janet scornfully replied, "There's always room for growth and always two sides to each story."

The next day, when Jay walked in to find Janet and myself at the table along with Ellie, he turned pale. He nodded at Janet. "Good morning." He nodded at Ellie. "Good morning." He tilted his chair so most of his back was toward me, boxing me out of the conversation. Ellie glanced at me in amazement.

During the course of the meeting, Jay rambled on about several incidents I had described to Ellie and Janet. Without even being asked, he defended himself in a way that confirmed my stories. When he started to go in the direction of blaming me for the extra work he had to do, Ellie said I had been following her orders. I couldn't believe she was finally standing up for me. He left after saying goodbye to both Ellie and Janet, ignoring me.

"Whoa, he walked right into that." Ellie said. "He confirmed everything Tali said."

Janet quickly turned toward Ellie, almost as if she was alarmed.

"I did not gather that at all," Janet replied. Her denial was a textbook example of the kind of gaslighting that eventually sent me over the edge. When Ellie tried to argue with her, Janet said, "We will not discuss this anymore. At the end of the day, our job is to please the client and none of this truly matters right now."

For the remainder of the day, I was given the grunt work. I had to pack up the office, do the final walk-through of the rooms, and collect meeting programs from seats. Jay became fast friends, hanging out and laughing the rest of the evening away.

During my corporate career, the need to constantly defend myself became emotionally taxing. I spent years stuck between a rock and hard place. Should I defend myself or not? What was the probability of reward vs. risk? Sadly, it was always the same. If I defended myself, it was the wrong choice. If I didn't defend myself, it was also the wrong choice.

I always paid a price.

10
A Candid Conversation with a Principal at a Top National Firm

Ryan Hayden
Principal at PwC
Boston, MA

Ryan Hayden is a prime example of the positive benefits that come from intentionally working to be an inclusive leader. It's not comfortable, and you will more than likely make some mistakes, but Ryan is proof that it can be done.

◆

Hopefully, by now you are convinced that bringing greater diversity and inclusion to your company is good for business and good for you. You see the necessity of taking action. But what kinds of steps will be necessary? This conversation with Ryan Hayden will give you a sense of what might be required of you as a leader. In a later chapter, an HR expert discusses the bigger picture of company-wide changes.

When I heard Ryan Hayden speak on a podcast about race relations in the workplace, I was impressed by his desire to know and be more when it came to being an inclusive leader. He is a respected principal at the professional services firm PricewaterhouseCoopers. There, he helps lead the company's national practice in healthcare, focused on risk with technology-enabled services. "In other words," said Ryan, "I'm a data geek who's worked in healthcare my whole life."

Having spent time in Africa and having married into an Indian family contributed to his awareness of the need to open up dialogue among members of different groups. He learned how genocide shaped Rwanda, how democracy in Botswana is creating the opportunity for change for women, and how the struggles for equality in South Africa still shape present-day politics, business, and everyday life. He's also aware of his wife's struggle to balance an appreciation for America's culture with a desire to instill Indian traditions in Ryan and their two children. "I've taken all of these personal observations, trips, reading, and family life and channeled it into how I lead as a Partner at the firm."

The Courage to Take a Risk

Ryan wanted to bring his staff together in conversations that would break down barriers, but he initially resisted taking responsibility for such a step. "I feared coming across as the prototypical alpha, white, wealthy male who had an agenda and was too aggressive and pushed his own way of engaging. I wanted it to be natural and organic. So I showed up and listened to others."

By confessing his fears about being overbearing, he gradually learned how to join his coworkers' conversations. "It brought about a tsunami of new ways to connect with people." There were pitfalls along the way. At one gathering, he asked several South Asian employees about their culture, which he was already familiar with, thanks to his wife's family. An observer judged his gesture as condescending to a minority group and reported the incident to Human Resources. The resultant inquiry was uncomfortable but enabled him to bring issues to the forefront in discussions throughout the company.

He has learned not to shy away from controversies that boil up in the public sphere. When a report was issued on racism in Boston, his company scheduled a two-hour session to discuss the topic. Five hundred people showed up. Hayden was one of a few administrators who broke the ice with their own stories of grappling with racial issues. He described the moment, soon after his first child's birth, when he was stunned to realize the challenges his biracial son might have to face. In the breakout groups that followed the leaders' stories, he met three staff members for the first time: a Dominican woman, an Asian American man, and an Eastern European woman. The stories they shared resulted in a bond among them, and they have remained in touch ever since.

A similar gathering followed a racially motivated shooting in Dallas. "You're not just monitoring the situation," Hayden explained, "but giving people the opportunity to grieve, share, talk about what it means to them. You create relationships through a set of shared experiences. There's a burden people carry that you can physically see when they let it go and see the reception people give them, of support, of hugs, of follow-ups, telling them they're not alone."

He offers advice for other white men who want to be allies but don't know how to get started: "Authenticity is key. People have to know you mean it. As well-intentioned as I have been, the topic is sticky and tough, and it's bound to produce unanticipated consequences. I've stepped in it." He asks people to help him learn if he's saying something wrong. "I have to be vulnerable and say I'm still learning," rather than avoid possibly awkward conversations.

11

Out of the Skillet and Into the Fire

I can't recall a time in corporate America that I was given the opportunity to do my job without being micromanaged, judged, dismissed, or taken advantage of. I've had to master the art of pretending that I was happy, although I was crying inside. So many of us have had to learn how to smile despite the pain, while continuing to offer our best work.

I arrived at the job interview fifteen minutes early. I wore a fitted black dress—not too fitted—with a tailored, black blazer. As usual, my hair was pulled back in a neat bun. A Black woman can never be sure her natural curls will be welcomed. I walked up to the receptionist with my head held high and a sincere smile on my face. I was excited about this position. It sounded like a chance to utilize my skills, meet lots of influential people, and bring my own creativity and ideas to the table.

"Hi, I'm here for an interview with Dr. Ausi."

The tiny receptionist behind the desk greeted me with a smile.

"Great! Please have a seat over there, and I'll let him know you're here." My heels clicked as I walked on the shiny, gray, glass tile floor, and she said, "I love your red bottoms. They are too cute."

Noticing the perplexed look on my face, she pointed down at my feet. "Your shoes, I really like them."

"Oh, thank you."

In hindsight, I wonder if she assumed that I was wearing the designer brand Christian Louboutin. At the time, I had never heard of them or the term *red bottoms*; I had purchased my shoes at Ross for $19.99.

"Talisa?" A short woman with curly, reddish hair called out to me.

"Yes, that's me." I was sure to smile as big as possible, as I didn't want there to be any chance that I was seen as unapproachable.

"I'm Shanna, Dr. Ausi's assistant. He's ready to see you."

I followed her down a long hall to Dr. Ausi's office. It had a traditional look, with dark wood furnishings, and trinkets from all over the world were scattered throughout.

"Well, you are a rock star! I couldn't wait to meet you."

A tall, slender, white man in a tailored, blue suit, with shiny black hair and extremely thin lips, greeted me in this unexpected way—with his hands held out and a grin on his face. His veneers were huge and extremely white. He spoke with a faint European accent.

I found myself literally looking around the room before replying, "Me?"

"Yes, you! I've been looking at your CV, and you are just what we need around here. Have a seat."

He introduced me to Diane, a plump, older white woman with short, gray hair and glasses. She gave me a half-smile. He explained that Diane would be working closely with me on planning events for the company, an educational facility.

The meeting lasted about fifteen minutes. They gave me a sketchy overview of the responsibilities the job entailed, while asking me only a very few general queestions. When they finished their presentation, I asked a few questions, ending with, "How soon do you expect to make your decision?"

"My mind is made up." Dr. Ausi flashed his shiny veneers and looked over at Diane as if he wanted her approval.

"Oh yeah, I think she's a great fit. I would love to work with you, Talisa." I was skeptical but so eager to leave the exasperating work situation I was in that I overlooked the bizarreness of the interview process. I convinced myself that they were offering me a dream job, a well-deserved miracle from the Universe. I could not deny this guy was weird, and yet I walked out of there knowing I would accept the job. Anything had to be better than where I was coming from.

Left On My Own

At the start of my first day of work, Maggie from HR handed me a stack of paperwork to fill out. When she walked me to my office, we were both surprised to find the door locked. Dr. Ausi was traveling, and his assistant didn't have the key. "Okay, I will need to find your key," Maggie said. "Just sit up front with Shanna for now."

"Sure," I replied, with my signature exaggerated smile.

I sat up front with Shanna for about an hour. I found her behavior odd. I soon realized that she was attempting to warn me that I was in for a rollercoaster with Dr. Ausi. I was so optimistic and excited that I decided that she was a negative person, and I'd be better off distancing myself from her.

The maintenance manager arrived to say he'd opened the door, and I asked Shanna what I should work on first. "I have absolutely no idea. I would say just go in there and dig around the files."

I looked through files, drawers, binders, books, and stacks of paper all day. I went back to Shanna for directions to Diane's office, and she gave me a map of the campus. I asked Shanna if I had an email account yet or if there were instructions for setting up my phone. She referred me to Maggie. Shanna soon made it clear I was bothering her and, oddly, Diane was nowhere near as friendly as she had been during our interview. When I asked to meet wit her, she blew me off and said we'd meet next week when Dr. Ausi returned. I ended up having to initiate the process of getting my own set of keys for the office. I also took a solo tour of the campus and went to introduce myself to people I'd researched on the company org chart. I even managed to get myself set up on the software and email server, and I located a warehouse that would house some of the props and decor that I would use for events.

I created a spreadsheet that listed all the vendors the previous planner worked with, and I sent them emails introducing myself. I felt proud for having the ability to jump right in and figure things out. I learned about an on-site event that was in the works, and I offered to help with the planning. Soon I had hired a florist and a caterer, and the arrangements were running along smoothly.

Disposable

It was Monday morning, and I was excited Dr. Ausi would be back in the office. I figured that it was good that I'd been able to familiarize myself with things before having our first official meeting. I drove to work that morning talking to a friend about how much I loved the job. I bragged about how resourceful I was and how I was already making huge progress with getting things organized. I never mentioned any of the weird behavior or negativity I was encountering. I was embracing a concept I'd recently encountered: the law of attraction. I was determined to focus on the positive. Finally, I had found the role that would work for me, and I refused to allow anything to stand in my way.

When I arrived, I went upstairs to the event space to meet with the caterer and florist. I was happy to find they had exceeded my expectations. I headed back down to my office, as we had a few hours before the start of the event. Maggie was standing at my door holding a binder. She smiled. "Good Morning. How are you?"

I smiled in return, "I'm excellent, how are you?"

"Not bad, where are you coming from?" I explained that I was preparing for today's event and that I had met with the caterer and florist. She looked surprised. "Oh wow! I didn't realize you were already in the planning phase."

I replied, "Yes ma'am, I jumped right in, headfirst."

"Well Dr. Ausi would like to meet with us this morning." I assumed that the look on her face was a hint that she didn't have the most positive feelings about Dr. Ausi, but at this point, my goal was to become one of his faves.

Dr. Ausi was seated behind his desk, typing on the computer. He didn't look up as we entered the room. "Is this still a good time?" Maggie asked as he glanced up, visibly annoyed. There was a long pause.

"Yes, give me just a sec, please." Maggie and I sat down at the table. It was a long, silent, and very awkward ten minutes as we waited for him to finish whatever he was doing on the computer.

Finally jumping up from his seat and flashing his veneers, he began to speak. "So, Talisa, you've had a week to get settled in, what do you think?"

I told him how much I'd accomplished and how great I felt about the job so far. Maggie maintained a subtle smile while nodding with approval as I spoke.

"Well, I'm glad you've enjoyed yourself, and I believe you when you say you've managed to pull so much off, but we're letting you go."

I felt like the wind had been knocked out of me.

"I'm sorry, what?!" My exaggerated smile went out the door.

"Yeah, it's nothing personal, and it's not about your work or anything. Think of it like dating. You meet someone, and you think there's a spark, and then after you spend some time with them, you realize...ah...maybe not so much. You get that, right?"

By now Maggie had resorted to a perfect poker face while avoiding any eye contact with me. It felt like I was having an out-of-body experience as I replied, "Dr. Ausi, with all due respect, no,

I don't get that. This is my career not my dating life, and I don't believe they are to be compared."

"Okay, maybe that was a bad analogy. Look at it like dancing. We dance a certain way here, and you have your own way of dancing, and it just doesn't flow." He looked over at Maggie, and she nodded. There was a long silence.

"I'm sorry, but I have never had a meeting with you. I had to set myself up on the operating systems, establish my own email account, make my own introductions, find my own key to my office—and you're telling me I'm fired because I can't dance? Dr. Ausi, I didn't sign up to work with a temp agency. I just resigned from my last job. I would appreciate it if you gave me more tangible facts regarding your decision to fire me."

Following another long and awkward pause, he threw his hands up in the air and said, "You're right! Forget what I said."

Now wanting to pinch myself to ensure that I was actually awake and that this was actually happening, I replied, "I'm sorry, what?"

"You are absolutely right. You have not had a chance to meet with me at all, and you at least deserve a chance to prove yourself. Again, I know you can do the job with your eyes closed. I have no doubt about that."

"Dr. Ausi, I need to know why this happened." Maggie frowned at me, almost as if she wanted to tell me to be quiet.

"Listen, don't worry about it. I own it. I made a mistake. Go get yourself a glass of water and relax. Forget this conversation ever happened."

To say that I was mortified is an understatement. I had no idea where this came from or who or what was behind it. I left his office with my hands shaking. I replayed the conversation I'd had with my friend earlier that morning, and I thought of how humiliating it would be to have to tell my friends and family that I once again needed to leave my job.

I sat at my desk. Before I could put my head down, Maggie walked in. "Are you okay?"

I couldn't believe she was asking me this question.

"No, I am absolutely not okay. What just happened?"

Maggie tried to look concerned. "Listen, he said don't worry about it. Sometimes we all make mistakes. I'm glad you're still here."

I fought back the tears. "Is this normal?"

Maggie seemed to be lost for words. Finally, she said, "No, seriously you are fine. Just relax, go to your car for a minute if you need to, and then come back. Don't let this affect how you do your job."

I grabbed a tissue as, against my will, my tears had escaped. I was angry at myself for crying, but I couldn't help it. "How am I supposed to go and do this event? It starts in twenty minutes. I honestly can't believe what just happened."

"Well, you told him how you felt, and he listened. I would say that's a good thing. I'm going now, so you can get yourself together in time to manage the event. Seriously, don't worry about it."

The next eight months were excruciating. Dr. Ausi was out for my blood, although the only difference between me and the other employees was the color of my skin. His aversion to me made me an easy target for bullying and abuse from other colleagues, and I didn't have a leg to stand on.

Stereotypes

I will never forget a meeting I attended where he and Diane were present. We were planning an off-site event, and Diane mentioned needing to get her husband something to wear. "May I bring a guest?" I asked. I didn't necessarily intend to bring anyone, but I wanted to be sure of the protocol.

Diane chuckled. "I mean, sure, as long as he doesn't have gold teeth and braids in his hair."

Lack of Trust

One of my tasks was to improve the school's annual conference. Dr. Ausi asked me to recruit a new marketing company to work on a rebrand and growth strategy for the event. Over several weeks, I spent hours looking through advertisements, websites, and LinkedIn profiles for the perfect company to partner with us in this endeavor. I read long proposals, compared stats, contacted references, and conducted interviews. I finally narrowed the field down to two companies that I planned to present to Dr. Ausi and the executive team. After telling him how and why I had chosen them, he asked me to place a hold on one of the companies and schedule a meeting with the other right away. This was a great decision, as far as I was concerned. I had built a great rapport with this team and felt it would be wonderful to work with them over the upcoming months as we planned the event. It was a local and highly praised Black-owned business.

The founder, Arnez, and his team arrived on time for the presentation, and I chatted with them as we waited for Dr. Ausi. The group praised my enthusiasm, research, communication, and knowledge of the conference. I deeply appreciated the validation.

Dr. Ausi and the executives made a grand entrance. Since I had spent several weeks doing research and developing a relationship with Arnez and his team, I expected to be the one to kick off the meeting. But Dr. Ausi barged ahead, addressing the team. "So, what do you have to offer that no one else can?"

Arnez gave his spiel, showing how knowledgeable they were about our organization, the conference, and our objectives for the coming year.

Dr. Ausi was condescending and insinuated more than once that he wasn't sure Arnez's company had the skill set or manpower to pull off the tasks he required. It was intriguing to see Arnez and his team hold their own. Their presentation was flawless and compared to the other offers that were on the table, they were certainly the best fit.

"Well, thank you all for coming by. We will consider your proposal and get back to you to let you know what we decide."

As we headed out of the boardroom, I felt embarrassed. Dr. Ausi didn't so much as acknowledge that I was in the room and acted as though I had not briefed him on the team's credentials.

The second option was a company owned by a white woman. At her presentation, it was obvious she had been in business a much shorter time, and her style didn't match the look and feel we were going for. Her fees were also 15 percent higher. Twenty minutes into the presentation, it was clear to me they were not the best choice for our marketing partner.

To my surprise, Dr. Ausi asked me to shortlist them and continue looking. Over several more weeks of research, we kept hitting brick walls. Dr. Ausi asked me to offer the white woman-owned business the job. With a broken heart, I made the call. I couldn't believe Arnez's company had been thrown out. They were beyond perfect, and this choice made no sense. But Dr. Ausi's choice was no longer able to accept the role, after all, because of prior engagement that they were committed to.

We, too, were at a point where we had to bring a marketing team in to help us with rebranding. Dr. Ausi reluctantly told me to hire Arnez and his team.

Arnez gladly accepted and soon discovered he had entered an agreement that would cause him a great deal of stress. Dr. Ausi micromanaged, insulted, gaslighted, and sabotaged the team repeatedly. He used them as scapegoats for anything that went wrong. He soon forbade me to talk to them; I felt he was suspicious of my cordial relationship with them. My removal from the process only added to the confusion and difficulty of properly executing the marketing plan.

I eventually left the company to pursue a healthier work environment. A year later, I reached out to Arnez and found out he was suing Dr. Ausi for the 50 percent of their fee he had refused to pay, as well as emotional distress

12

An Important Confession

I have to admit that in the past, I've failed to be attentive to my fellow marginalized colleagues. It's easy to become engulfed in our own reality while failing to see that others are dealing with similar plights that could very well require similar remedies.

To other marginalized groups of people that I have encountered in my career, this confession is to you.

There is a great deal of danger that comes with ignoring and chastising marginalized groups of people. I have to admit, it's only recently that I've noticed you. Before now, I saw you as someone separate from me. It wasn't a conscious thought. It's not like I walked past you and thought, they're not like me, but when I really sat down and began to think through the issues that I wanted to address in this book, I also wanted to understand the issues that plagued all marginalized people in general. Understanding and reflecting upon the perplexities that you face within the workplace allows me to experience what white people must feel like when thinking about the issues that I present from a Black woman's perspective. Racism runs deep, but there are other human traits that make people see each other differently: age, disability, sexuality, and religion to name a few. Amongst groups that are denied involvement or fair treatment in mainstream activities, there is a great deal of potential for us to bond—a relationship we haven't fully taken advantage of.

The Reality of Numbers

Merriam-Webster defines a minority as "the smaller number or part, especially a number that is less than half the whole number."

It's clear that a small group of people are going to face a massive challenge if their members try to change the attitudes and behavior of a larger group of people. Only when members of the larger group are motivated to participate in change does real progress happen.

At the onset of the 2020 Black Lives Matter movement, I was amazed by the crowds of white people who went out to protest police brutality against the Black community. After decades of failure on the part of the authorities to take substantial action to address the scourge of racially motivated killings by police, it felt as though progress was finally being made. I view the white allies who have joined the movement as wind beneath our wings.

What if the members of various minority groups banded together to support each other? Our numbers would swell, and even if we couldn't collectively add up to a majority, our voice would be louder than the voice of any individual group. We may not all have the same struggles, but we know what it is to be dismissed and excluded. With women being a minority in business, I have two strikes against me as a Black woman. Others may have age, sexuality, or disability added to the mix—characteristics that even white men may share. We all need to acknowledge each other.

Sadly, much of the world rejects the notion that racism, sexism, ageism, ableism, homophobia, and more exist in the workplace. The problems are masked by strategic efforts to hire people who can boost a firm's diversity numbers, especially if they can put an extra woman, a person of color, or a person with a visible disability in the company photo. Meanwhile, the behavior of coworkers continues to damage our self-esteem and prevent us from offering our best selves on the job.

The obstacles we face are systemic. I'm working overtime to convince those in power to initiate change. But change has to come from all levels. I know we are exhausted and just want to go to work, but inclusion begins with us. We, too, have to work hard on facing, admitting, and removing our own biases. If we learn to empathize with others and their struggles, we can move mountains. Much of my book speaks about my own experience as a Black woman, but my desire is to be a voice and champion for anyone struggling to be valued, respected, and appreciated in the workplace.

My Proposal for Atonement and Reconciliation

Through education and a sincere desire to see beyond ourselves, we can create bonds across groups that could create positive changes for us all. Seek out other marginalized voices and perspectives. Go online and look for activists, bloggers, authors, artists, and other voices from marginalized communities. Their personal stories and experiences will teach, outrage, and inspire you, while showing you how much we have in common.

Open your mind and your ears. Be willing to spend time with people who are different from you, even if it means you have to be uncomfortable for a while. Accept that you will make mistakes. Be willing to be wrong and be willing to hear how you can be better moving forward. Becoming defensive or holding a grudge is counterproductive to progress.

Hold the people in your life accountable. Confront people who exhibit behaviors derived from hate or ignorance. Realize there is nothing entertaining about jokes that demean minorities. What may feel like lighthearted fun could be an element of oppression. As we seek to evolve, being complicit should no longer be acceptable.

Let's commit to actually seeing, hearing, and understanding one another. I am not separate from you, and you are not separate from me. We need each other now more than ever. If we choose to be dismissive or complicit because it's not our issue, we only contribute to the bleak circumstance that we all face. Let's all be willing to grow while contributing to positive change.

13

Barack Obama And The End Of My Career

For years, I dreamed of escaping corporate America and pursuing en-
trepreneurship. I made several attempts, but the lack of start-up capital
and support was always a deterrent. I would have never predicted the
series of events that caused me to feel as though I had no choice but to
walk away. I wasn't sure that I'd manage to ever be a successful entre-
preneur, but I was sure that I'd reached a breaking point that would
change my life forever.

◆

"**G**reat news, team! We finally secured our speaker for
the upcoming event. I am proud to announce that
former President Barack Obama said YES! Thanks so much for
all of your hard work thus far. We look forward to supporting you
as we pull this wonderful engagement together, and we know that
you will make us proud."

My heart began to race. I couldn't believe my eyes. I read the
message over and over again, trying to convince myself that this was
actually happening. I screamed with excitement. I knew this was a
game changer, and it would be the absolute highlight of my career.

I was sitting in a boutique luxury resort, in the Outer Banks
of Southern California, when the notification popped up on my

phone. I was on an advance site visit for another event. We typically spent two or three days at the location, and if the event was to be at a hotel or resort, the staff would go above and beyond with their customer service, in an attempt to knock our socks off. They would offer us the best views, leave us personalized cards, send up bottles of wine at the end of the day, and it wasn't out of the norm for them to surprise us with desserts and even trinkets and gifts to take home. We would taste several items from the menu throughout the day, including wine, beer, and cocktails. We would go out and explore the surrounding area, visit local restaurants and attractions, and get to know other local vendors and partners we would potentially work with to pull off the event. It wasn't very often that I was allowed to go on site visits, at least not in comparison with others in my position. It was always a treat to be able to go.

As soon as the message arrived, I reached out to my closest friends and family members to share my excitement and pride about planning an event where Barack Obama would be the keynote speaker.

As dinnertime approached, I decided that I would have a small bottle of champagne and a piece of gourmet chocolate cake with raspberry topping. I was not concerned about my diet that night.

I hadn't been with this company long, and it was a bit of luck that I'd fallen into such an amazing opportunity.

While waiting on dinner to be delivered, I hopped in the shower. After such a long and eventful day, I embraced the opportunity to massage and cleanse my shoulders with the disposable sea sponge provided by the resort. The warm water and lush, creamy soap ran down my body, and I was intentionally present and savoring the moment. Comparable to an alarm clock, my internal dialogue caused me to awaken from my state of bliss. *This assignment is going to be the death of your career at this company, and you know that Lana has shown you several signs of disloyalty. Why would you trust her? Who are you kidding?* Her reassurance means nothing. Feeling my enthusiasm beginning to waver, I remembered my decision to stay positive and pushed the thought away. I was confident in my abilities, and this event was a chance of a lifetime. It belonged to me.

Later that evening, I sat on my balcony in my PJs, listening to the tunes of Sarah Vaughn and watching the sun disappear into the ocean. With my tummy full of steak and potatoes and my mind still and filled with gratitude, I enjoyed every bite of my gourmet chocolate cake with raspberry topping, and every slow sip of my crisp berry champagne. I'll never forget the feeling I had when I laid my head on the pillow that night. Things were finally beginning to fall into place for me.

"Oh my God, Barack Obama! I'm so jealous," my sister exclaimed as I shared the news.

"Don't be jealous, I can't wait to get my picture with him, I'm so excited!"

"Yeah, this is a really big deal. To be able to say that you worked with him. Good for you."

When I returned from my trip, the news had begun to float around the office. I knew from experience that when it came to communicating with my colleagues, it would not be received well if I showed too much excitement about the opportunity to plan—let alone lead—an event featuring Barack Obama. I witnessed others discussing their involvement. Their announcements were met with mutual excitement. It hurt to see my colleagues celebrate and be celebrated, while I had to contain my enthusiasm or risk them rolling their eyes at what a novice I was, as if someone with my experience shouldn't make a big deal about working with former President Obama.

Hard Work Pays Off, Or Does It?

Planning this event robbed me of three months of my life. I'm not exaggerating. I worked constantly, never closing my laptop before midnight. My weekends were no longer for leisure. There was always something more that needed to be done. I worked harder than I've ever worked to pull this event together. In hindsight, I realize that a great deal of the hard work and sleepless nights was a result of being mistreated. Lana, the only other Black event manager out of a department of over one-hundred people, was supposed to oversee me while I led the event, but about a month before the scheduled date, Lana and upper management decided we would co-lead the event together. I had no problem with this decision, as she had been with the company for about three years and had experience working with the client; they seemed more receptive to her communication. She was also an extreme micromanager, so I looked forward to splitting tasks down the middle and taking ownership of my own pieces of the puzzle while still having a grasp of the full picture.

A few weeks before the event was to take place, I started to receive subtle hints that I might be removed from the assignment, although none of the reasons I heard made any sense at all. Lana was suddenly so busy that she could barely speak to me. I was was approached by management and reprimanded about conversations that had never taken place. I was held accountable for dialogue presented in meetings that I had never attended or even been invited to.

The mental games, collective efforts to sabotage my work, and gaslighting attempts were staggering.

A week before the event, I was pulled into a meeting where I learned that record would reflect I assisted on a very small portion of the event. I read between the lines and realized that much of the work that I'd done to prepare for the meeting had been hijacked by Lana and presented as if I had nothing to do with it.

Temp workers and people who had been pulled in at the last minute were praised, while I was ignored and treated as if I had not worked as the manager of the event. Even worse, people behaved as if I was not in the room. I felt debilitated. I knew that if I said a single word or even breathed too loud, I would be removed from the planning and execution of the event. After all the sleepless nights and sacrifices I had made to help pull this event off, I was determined to be there and reap the rewards of planning an event highlighting former President Barack Obama.

Three days before the event, I was reluctantly given the green light to purchase my plane ticket. When I read a group email with details regarding hotel rooms for staff, I saw that my name had been left off the list. Someone was determined to keep me from attending this event. When I think back on that time, it feels like I was running a mental and emotional intelligence obstacle course. For weeks, I had countless opportunities to lose my cool, but I refused to give in. I politely asked questions about my absence from the report and watched a few different people in management skate around answers while blaming each other.

The day had finally come. I was on the airplane with a hotel confirmation in my name. I gave myself pep talks the whole way there. Despite the tumultuous journey, I was excited and ready to execute a dynamic event. I would go on-site, I would work diligently, and I would leave with the ability to tell future employers that I had planned and executed an event where former President Barack Obama was the keynote speaker.

The Big Day

I stood in the back of the hall, clipboard in hand, watching the four hundred guests trickle in and find their seats at the big, round tables, draped with tablecloths that gleamed snowy white beneath the elegant arrangements of pink and red flowers. The murmuring voices conveyed an air of excitement that I embraced. Former President Barack Obama would soon make his way to the dais, and I would see him and hear him speak. I had made it. They couldn't take the prize away from me now.

Then I saw a colleague, Fran, heading toward me with a sour look on her face, and I felt a lurch in my stomach. I'd met her only once before. I'll never forget walking into a room where she was discussing a rapper and his decision to speak out about racism. She expressed her disgust with his choice to *pull the race card*. She was convinced that whatever he was griping about had nothing to do with anyone being racist, and everything to do with his own behavior. Taken aback by her statements, I realized I needed to be extremely careful around her.

I'd seen her in the hotel lobby when I arrived, and she had ignored my attempt to greet her. Now she approached me at the peak of the event. The event I had worked on for months. The event she had taken no part in planning. She told me I was managing the catering process all wrong and that she was working with the kitchen to fix it. In fact, there was nothing wrong with the catering or the process. She would eventually say there was an issue with the timing of their placement of dishes. She didn't realize the timing was purposely delayed because the Secret Service would not allow the kitchen staff to move when Obama was in the process of entering or leaving the building.

Executives would later argue that she was within her rights to tell me whatever she wanted to tell me and in any fashion that she wanted to tell me, because despite the fact that I had coordinated time lines with the kitchen and Secret Service, she knew what the company wanted and how the company wanted things to be done. My choice to assure her that everything was fine, and that I'd meticulously managed the process, caused her to report that my response and tone had been disrespectful and unacceptable. There were no witnesses to this exchange, but her falsified rendition of the incident was accepted as truth. I was told I needed to accept it or it would further damage me, since I had not only failed to do my job correctly but I had been disrespectful to a colleague—and now I was being defensive.

During the event, the clients praised me repeatedly and quickly grew to depend on me for a number of last-minute requests and changes. I barely had a moment to catch my breath that day, but I felt it was an honor and nothing within me wanted to complain. While others had their photos taken with the former president, I was told I couldn't even snap a photo of him with my cell phone. What should have been the peak moment of my career ended up being the bitter end.

The events leading up to my decision to walk away from corporate America echoed every offense that I have described in this book, and more; colleagues comforted me only in private. Others spoke up and were silenced. White women banded together in support of each other and against me, despite their lack of awareness or any of the facts presented. The CEO, who talked a huge game about being an inclusive leader and running an equitable company, backed me and then bolted. I could go on and on. I saw with excruciating clarity that I would always be acting in the same drama, with different players, in a different setting, during a different year. But this particular incident was so extreme that I could not continue to pretend that my life within the meetings and event industry was suitable. After all, I'd been warned that young, cute, skinny, blue-eyed, blonde-haired, and big-boobed was the winning formula. I surrendered.

I have come to a bold conclusion that everything about this moment aligned with the vicious cycle, that I felt trapped within for years, qualifies me to be the author of this book. Black women are suffering in corporate America. Other marginalized groups are suffering as well. The pain is deeper than most people want to acknowledge. After a decade of anguish, I dejectedly raised my white flag. I had tried every recourse I could think of, and nothing worked. I could no longer see myself struggling to survive, much less attempting to scramble toward the top.

I walked away from the career that had held all my hopes and inspired so much hard work. I had no idea how I would take care of myself, and I didn't care. The only thing I was sure of was that I had nothing left to give. I had hit rock bottom, and my pain outweighed my ability to see any future worth pursuing.

14

A Candid Conversation with a Human Resources and Affirmative Action Expert

Terri Swain
The HR Consultant
Dallas, TX

Terri Swain understands the importance of diversity, equity and inclusion in the workplace. Sharing stories with her is always a validating experience. She has witnessed the dysfunction that comes with organizations that attempt to ignore disparities. Terri is someone that we can all learn from.

◆

As you have gathered by now, making change at the company level is not a simple endeavor. But it's worth doing, and it's possible to do, if leaders take responsibility for an initiative that's both focused and comprehensive. I invited Human Resources expert Terri Swain to describe some of the pitfalls and explain what it takes to carry out a successful transformation.

"Overcoming barriers to discrimination in the workplace is a leadership issue," Terri said, "and there are things that leaders must do to make it happen. I've seen it succeed. I've also seen what happens when you don't have effective leadership."

Terri has experienced the field from all sides of the table: government, corporate, court, and consulting. She has worked as a United States Equal Employment Opportunity Commission investigator and as Fortune 200 HR Leader in Affirmative Action.

In 1998, she started her own firm, The HR Consultant, which addresses harassment and discrimination through training, affirmative action planning, third-party investigation, and expert witness testimony at trials. "I see the statistics. I've investigated the stories," she said. "I understand the issues and the mountains people are up against trying to fight discrimination and harassment in the workplace."

Motivation

When a company decides to work toward an environment that supports diversity and harmony among all its employees, the leadership must ask themselves, "Are we doing this to look good or to appease a particular group of employees/leaders/investors? Or are we truly doing this because we understand there is strength in diversity?"

Terri said leaders who can answer these questions correctly have a good chance at success if they follow through with appropriate actions. The wrong answers lead to disaster.

Company X, for example, hired her firm as a result of losing an Equal Employment Opportunity Commission (EEOC) lawsuit. According to Terri, only 2 percent of all EEOC charges result in a negative finding. Far fewer advance to lawsuits, and yet fewer make it to a courtroom trial. "So, when a company gets an adverse finding through the courts, it's a pretty big deal," said Terri. "As part of the agreement with the Commission, they were required to pay out money to the plaintiffs and also conduct training, which we helped deliver."

At the beginning of the training, no leader was present to kick off the sessions. It was clear the company's sole motivation was to comply with the EEOC ruling. "As you can imagine, there wasn't much engagement from the audience," Terri recalled. "It was obvious they didn't understand the problem they had created in their organization or how to fix it. That company is no longer in business."

In contrast, Company A is a large consumer products firm that was having issues at a plant in a small Texas town. The facility was an acquisition, and headquarters was receiving multiple racial and sexual discrimination charges, lawsuits, and internal complaints. "The company's approach to it was one that exemplifies leadership and a willingness to examine the organization and change," said Terri.

The first step was the assembling of focus groups that included outside consultants, Terri among them. The company insisted on a racially diverse team of consultants, which proved invaluable. Members of the consulting team were able to observe differences in treatment of the white and non-white consultants in the community, outside of the workplace. This observation was critical to understanding the extent of the problem and how it would be necessary to reach beyond the four walls of the company to impact change.

Without a strong commitment from leadership, this first step would not have been so productive.

A Holistic Approach

Terri has also encountered companies where their idea of progress is to recruit for diversity, or provide diversity training, or create employee resource groups or a diversity council, but they lack a comprehensive strategy. "These companies don't understand that a holistic approach is necessary. Otherwise, these activities are viewed as 'flavors of the month' without any real teeth."

In focus groups and interviews at Company Y, work/life balance was identified as a top diversity issue. "But the Senior HR leader in that organization said, 'We are doing diversity. We're not doing work/life balance.' He wanted to attack the issue through his own perceptions rather than listening to the feedback of many employees." The organization was successful at recruiting diverse hires but could not retain them because the corporate culture was too demanding of their time, as later turnover analysis and exit interviews showed. They poured money into recruiting and paying diverse employees but were not able to keep them.

Back at Company A, employee feedback showed Terri's team that the barriers to equality were both psychological and physical. The plant workers were racially diverse, but the management staff was mostly white and male. Management was housed in an area that workers could not access without a solid reason, while managers rarely came into the plant unless there was a problem. "In an environment where you don't have physical access to decision makers or see any that look like you," said Terri, "combined with a community that doesn't embrace diversity, it was easy to see how this environment was ripe for complaints."

With the leadership committed to decisive, clear action, Company A responded on multiple fronts.

First, a management reorganization brought in staff from within the larger organization who were willing to listen and communicate. To ensure a transition to a more diverse management team, succession planning and career development programs were instituted to groom high-potential minority and female employees.

The workspace was reconfigured to allow more contact between management and plant workers.

Terri's firm was utilized as a third party to hear treatment complaints.

High levels of corporate and local management kicked off the first training program. Instead of jumping straight into diversity training, the initial program paved the way with "Creating a Respectful Work Environment," with attendance by all managers, supervisors, and employees. Once the basics of respect were communicated and embraced, trainings could move on to more sophisticated diversity concepts.

The topic did not stop at the doors of the plant but was brought into conversations in the community.

Communication

Company A was a major player in the small town and succeeded in influencing suppliers, civic leaders, and newspapers to join in the discussions.

Employee surveys and focus groups became a part of their culture as the company continued to self-evaluate. Employees with complaints were taken seriously and responded to, which made them feel free to speak up. As issues were resolved, the number of complaints fell. Managers who were open to suggestions and created clear communication channels were rewarded. At the same time, the succession plan resulted in diversity within the management sector.

"This was a company that recognized that when you have a number of employee complaints, it's a clear signal that something is wrong," said Terri. "And they realized that solving the problem required a long-term, thoughtful approach."

While consultants can help a company straighten out their diversity issues, it's ultimately up to the leadership to make sure the effort succeeds.

15

A Sincere Confession

When working in the coveted meetings and events industry, I was always a token Black. I was never able to master being the ideal token, but I desperately wanted to. I now realize that I subconsciously owned it and wore it like a badge of honor. If I had known then what I know now, I would have handled things much differently.

◆

To the other Black women that I've worked with over the years, this is my confession to you.

It's unfortunate that many of us have allowed those in power to turn us against one another. I can remember a few times when you preceded me and walked around as though you had conquered the land and taken your throne. You made it obvious there wasn't room for both of us, and you refused to allow me to threaten your coveted place. You aligned yourself with white women that were blatantly intolerant and manipulative, even at the expense of your own dignity.

You've been candid with me about your fears while pretending to be an ally. I remember asking you to join me for lunch, and you hesitated to accept my invitation. Finally, you said, "That's fine, but no one here can know we're going together. I will meet you at the restaurant." I understand where you're coming from, and you're right: if the only two Black women in the company become close friends, white people tend to display their discomfort; if feels as though they assume that we're somehow up to no good or plotting to do something sinister. We'll be seen as excluding them, creating our own little dominion, sadly increasing their baseless suspicions of us. It's just another reason that your next promotion, as well as mine, would be in jeopardy. Both concerned and rightfully so, we've allowed their insecurities and passive manipulation to keep us from supporting each other.

I've always envied those of you who could play the game so well. If only I had what it took to be in their good graces the way you are. I've hated the fact that I've annoyed even you, and that you felt the need to separate yourself from me.

You've mastered the art of pretending things are not really that hard for us. When I was younger, I believed there was a certain kind of Black woman who was well received in corporate America. After all, you helped them push this narrative. It wasn't until I checked all the boxes and still found myself demeaned that I realized you had become accustomed to putting on an act. You, too, were suffering on the inside while flaunting the perks that you barely had access to.

We Can All Change

I've struggled with viewing you as an enemy. I've wanted to trust you and to genuinely bond with you. The walls between us have made this impossible. Let's take a look at the bigger picture. We all desire equality in the workplace, but if we are honest, we have also subconsciously played a part in the deep-rooted, institutionalized racism that is currently running rampant in corporate America. Our desire to appear less threatening to our white colleagues has caused us to make it easier for them to treat us disproportionately. The world is now challenging privileged white people to stand up and use their voices. There has never been a better time for *us* to act differently, to think differently, and to no longer accept the unspoken role of dismissing and tearing each other down.

Professionalism is necessary in the workplace. But we have to challenge what *professionalism* looks and acts like. For too long we have accepted the idea that being professional means assimilating into white cultures. In the end, this belief has damaged us and our race as a whole.

I've seen the regret in your eyes as you threw me underneath the bus; You were torn between doing what was right, at the risk of backlash, and doing what you felt you had to do in order to protect your own livelihood and the well-being of your family. Many times, you would call me foolish when I was determined to do what was morally right. You knew my choice would rouse the anger of the powers that be. Often, doing the right thing wasn't in the best interest of the white-washed teams that held my future in their hands. Sometimes doing the right thing caused a light to shine on the dysfunction that so many had grown accustomed to pretending wasn't there.

I realize that despite your title and the position that you seem to hold, you feel powerless, and you are doing the best that you can. I have no desire to task you with more action items regarding your professionalism or skills. As you forge your way into the companies of those who don't look, talk, or act like you, I hope they have better equipped themselves with knowledge that allows them to see you. To see your color, to see your hair, to see your lips, to see your humanness.

Whether you're currently working in a service role or have a job as a factory worker, a teacher, a medical professional, or you find yourself sitting in the boardroom trying to navigate your way to the top—I extend my solidarity and support to you. I know the struggles you encounter from day to day. I am recognizing you and pushing your plight to a space within the collective narrative about the injustices that Black Americans endure from day to day.

You, too, are worthy of a life that doesn't include humiliation, microaggression, and the constant threat of losing both your moral compass and your job. You are worthy of being more than a pawn or the solution for a previously abandoned checkbox. You deserved to be legitimately hired for the talents you can offer an organization, and you deserve to work without feeling as though you have to abandon the truth of who you are.

My Proposal for Atonement and Reconciliation

Hold tightly to your self-worth. Remember you may not always be able to find the validation you crave to assure yourself that you're not losing your mind and that you didn't do anything wrong. Unfortunately, oppressors are everywhere, and they sit in the trenches waiting for the perfect opportunity to label you an angry Black woman.

I propose that we all acknowledge in our hearts who we really are, while gradually learning to respond authentically to the world and work environments that we are placed in. Little by little and day by day, let's make a commitment to revealing our true selves and supporting each other along the way. No longer should we be afraid to discuss who we are, even when our interests are not aligned with mainstream white patterns and trends. We, too, have a responsibiity to change the norm by being bold enough to unapologetically be ourselves.

Together, we can vow to quit accepting and playing into the unspoken bias that comes with befriending other Black women at work. We have to hold ourselves accountable while remembering that yielding to that pressure may feel like the most comfortable option in the moment, but it is counterproductive to our overall progress. We are so much stronger together—and together, in due time, we will prevail.

16

My Name Is Not Beyoncé

I suffered from the same thorn in my side for years, with no resolution in sight, until I was catapulted out of the corporate world into a place of devastation. It was during my lowest moment that a revelation presented itself and gave an overarching meaning and purpose to my life.

My skin felt clammy and cold, my mouth was dry, and my limbs ached. The air smelled stale, and beeping sounds pierced my ears. I looked around, wondering where I was and what had happened. When I tried to sit up, I realized I was tied to a bed. It wasn't my bed, and the clothes I was wearing were not mine.

Then it hit me. I was still alive.

How the hell is this even possible? I took so many pills, and I drank so much wine. Who brought me here? How long have I been here? Where are my clothes?

"Talisa, you can't get up. Relax. You're at Thompson Hospital."

I can't get up? What the fuck?

"How did I get here?"

"You were brought in by ambulance about four hours ago." A middle-aged white woman, with a huge, black mole on her top lip and long, salt-and-pepper hair, stood over me as I struggled to understand my reality. She was matter-of-fact, frowning, and indifferent. For a split second, I wondered if perhaps I had been successful and was dead and in hell after all.

"I need to go to the restroom. Please untie me." I tugged at the restraints.

"No, you can't do that. I'll bring you a bedpan."

"I'm not using a bedpan. Let me out of here!" At this point, my objective was to call a Lyft and get back home. There, I would finish what I'd started, and I would certainly be successful this time.

The vibration from my cell phone startled me. It was my friend Keanna. I managed to answer the phone and put it on speaker.

"Tali, where are you? Are you okay?"

"Who did this? How did I get here?"

"A few of us made calls and realized you were not okay."

"I don't want to be here. I'm getting out of here and going home to finish what I started."

"Oh no! You can't do that. Why would you hurt me that way? You are being extremely selfish right now!"

I hung up the phone. I didn't want to hear it.

Despite the nurse insisting I use the bedpan, I refused. I eventually managed to talk her into allowing me to use the toilet while she supervised.

When I was moved to another room, still shackled, I discovered stickers on my chest and bruises all over my body. I must have struggled against ambulance personnel. I'd been given an EKG test and poked multiple times with needles. I had no recollection of those four hours, including the removal from my apartment.

It quickly became apparent that the hospital had no intention of letting me go. I figured maybe I'd have to stay one night. I gave myself pep talks about how I would go home tomorrow, and life would be over soon.

As more and more concerned family and friends reached out to me on my cellphone, my only objective was getting to the bottom of who exactly sounded the alarm that landed me in the hospital. I made it clear that I resented their interference, and they made it equally clear that they didn't care about my resentment. I felt betrayed.

Rock Bottom Has a Basement

When I walked away from what I knew would be my last attempt at being a corporate event manager, my boyfriend, the love of my life, refused to let me fall apart about making that final break. He insisted we celebrate and assured me I had what it takes to finally become an entrepreneur—especially with the emotional and financial support he would offer. While I appreciated his gestures and agreed to engage in a celebratory outing with him, there was still a part of me that was nursing the grief of a dream unfulfilled.

I had worked hard to make a success of that relationship, a major accomplishment for me. He had presented an opportunity for me to learn to be okay with being dependent on another person for once. He called me his Princess. I finally felt like I was in a position to approach the rest of my life with a partner.

A week later, he informed me that he could no longer see me; all the financial and emotional support I needed more than ever was officially off the table.

The Antagonizer Within

"He left, and now I'm leaving." I texted my friend as I started to drink a second full bottle of Merlot.

"Who left? Leaving to go where?"

"Let my little sister know that I love her. I'm too ashamed to tell her goodbye."

"Tali, what the fuck are you talking about? Where are you, what's going on? What happened?"

"David left me. His ex called him, and she needs him, and he's sorry. We just had the best Halloween, we had a room booked for Thanksgiving, and I was supposed to fly home with him to meet his family for Christmas. He was going to help me reach my entrepreneurial goals. I believed him. I loved him and he just left. I have no job, no plan, no support, no love, I have nothing and no one. I can't live like this."

"No, Tali! No! That's it, I'm calling the police."

The Time I Flew Over the Cuckoo's Nest

"Why is Beyoncé sitting on the floor crying?"

"Carla, be quiet and mind your own business."

"Sorry, but when you see Beyoncé in the psych ward, sitting on the floor crying, you wonder why." Carla was a short, Hispanic woman in her early twenties. She had long, black hair and an innocent look on her acne-scarred face. She was wearing brown scrubs, identical to the ones they'd given me when I arrived. I had been transported by ambulance to Naveaux, a new facility. I was clueless about what I'd gotten myself into. I sat on the cold floor and wept. Several other patients walked past me and speculated while people in authority told them to stop.

"How ya feeling, Talisa?" one of the male staff asked.

"I'm ready to go home," I mumbled.

He smirked. "Yeah, right. You may as well make yourself comfortable. You won't be getting out of here anytime soon." His statement was alarming. It triggered a memory from the phone conversation I'd had with Keanna while tied down to that bed at Thompson.

"You better stop being rude to those people, or you will never get out of there." My friend's warning came in response to my complaint about being forced to use a piece of thick paper, instead of a fork, to eat my eggs and pancakes. I wanted to scream and demand that they let me out, but I listened to her words. There was so much to be learned about navigating my way out of that place. Her pep talk made me realize it would be in my best interest to keep my frustrations at bay. I also knew I had to keep my strong, lingering desire to complete my suicide a secret.

I stayed at Naveaux for the longest and most miserable week and a half of my life. Most of the inmates were people who were not only a danger to themselves but also a danger to others, many of them mired in psychosis, most of them delusional. Carla literally believed I was Beyoncé.

I often couldn't hear what people were saying to me, as there was always someone screaming, banging on walls, or singing at the top of their lungs. Many of the inmates had no homes, so they thought of Naveaux as a safe place. It was a private facility that earned funds for every person it housed, so there was a clear incentive to keep patients there as long as possible. Once I understood the politics of the place, my thought process began to change. Both the machinations of the administration and the disdain from the staff reminded me of the corporate society I had left behind, and this sense of recognition not only outraged me, it also pulled me back to myself. I feared that if I didn't find a way to get out of there soon, I would descend into real madness. I had to shake myself back into a state of reality, a state that I had so desperately wanted to escape. I had to dig deep and gain conscious access to all my mental faculties so that I could think rationally and strategically about how to get myself out of there. I also struggled with the awareness that if I was serious about killing myself, maybe I did belong there. As the hours passed, my determination to complete my plan for suicide subsided. Only then did I feel comfortable enough to reach out to my loved ones.

One day, Carla gave me a red notebook and a few tiny pencils with thick erasers attached. She had won them in a Bingo game a few weeks before. "I can tell you really want to write," she said mysteriously. By this time, I think she realized I wasn't Beyoncé.

That notebook was a life saver. I wrote in it day and night, going to the receptionist to have my little pencils sharpened several times a day.

One of the entries from the notebook will always stick with me:

This place is filled with some of the most interesting characters I've ever encountered, but it all reminds me of corporate America. From the frivolous water cooler chats, to the people who love it here and play the game like nobody's business, to the people in authority that I could literally run circles around. They treat me like trash. They have no idea that less than a month ago I was flying business class with a corporate card and laptop to go and work on an event with Barack Obama. They are so dismissive and condescending yet they hold the key to my existence outside of these walls. I have to play the game if I want to ever get out of here with my sanity intact. I am forcing myself to eat the gross food and smile when I'm greeted. I even went to play bingo yesterday. I hate it. I don't belong here. I don't belong here. I don't belong here....

The Turning Point

Within a few days, the staff started to acknowledge that I was not psychotic after all. Some even admitted they felt sorry for people like me, who had been dumped in such a grim place following a suicide attempt. I earned their trust and worked at making them my allies.They helped me strategize my way out of there.

It wasn't without a great deal of "playing the game" that I was finally released to go home. It was a bittersweet moment, since the life I was returning to was in shreds. But while writing in the note book, I had come to insights that gave me new inspiration. One, I would never again make my livelihood dependent on pretending to be someone I wasn't. Two, I had a new job to do. I had a story to tell, and that story could fuel changes that would not only benefit myself as I pursue wholeness and healing but would benefit others that are experiencing similar injustices. For too long I had allowed myself to be reduced to and viewed as a diverse hire, that should feel privileged to have the job while being dedicated to appeasing my bigoted peers. Instead of working for people within corporate America that dismissed me, I would position myself to work alongside them to remove their rose-colored glasses and transform their organizations from the inside out.

The breakdown I had suffered was not the end of my life. Instead, it was the catalyst for the creation of my very own platform that would finally allow me to do my job, to be myself, and to wear a genuine smile.

The work has just begun. Nothing brings me more joy than showing up as my whole self to break down barriers, expose broken systems, and initiate real change.

THE END

Epilogue

I didn't recognize the caller ID, but the unfamiliar voice on the phone asked, "Is this Talisa?"

"Yes."

"I'm so glad I found you. This is Sheila. Remember me from Blue Coast Mortgage Company?"

We hadn't talked in years. "Yes Sheila, of course I remember you. How are you?"

"I'm fine. I called to tell you something I knew you would want to hear." I was intrigued. "First of all, you were right. Oh my God, were you right! Are you sitting down?"

Sheila went on to remind me of the hell I went through while working at Blue Coast as a result of my direct report, a straight white man who did not bother to hide his racism or his sexism. Once he openly and jokingly discussed how Blacks would bring down the property value of homes when they moved into predominantly white neighborhoods. He made several sexual advances toward me, although I'd been vocal about how uncomfortable his crass comments made me feel. I was too young to realize that the gaslighting and insults I endured under his leadership would be classified as psychological abuse.

He was a much older man who eventually began to show signs of dementia. His mental vacations from reality were the bane of my existence. He would instruct me to do something and later reprimand me for it.

I found myself having to fight for my livelihood, and it was his word against mine. I pleaded my case while showing evidence of his racism, sexism, lack of professionalism, and dementia. I remember the looks on the faces of the people in Human Resources. I may as well have been speaking to a wall. The facts I presented didn't matter. He was a white man with a title. I was just a young Black girl with a southern accent.

Sheila was anxious to inform me that this man had recently been discovered in his home, dead. His wife and two dogs were also dead. The police report stated that after being laid off from his job, he packed up his belongings and stopped at a Chinese restaurant to pick up dinner for himself and his wife. They ate the meal together in bed. Then he shot his wife in the head, followed by the two dogs and then himself.

Hearing Sheila tell this story caused a flood of emotions. Like everyone else I worked with at that time, Sheila wasn't much of an ally or support to me as I battled to hang on to my livelihood and respect. Now she was going out of her way to deliver what felt like long overdue vindication and validation for all I suffered as a result of the biases I found myself up against, day after day.

I always knew I was right. She said she'd known I was right, too. But most of the time, being right isn't enough. Being right doesn't matter. In fact, being right and knowing you're right only adds insult to injury.

When I shared this story with a friend, she observed how ironic it was that a murder-suicide was such a turning point for me, and then later in life, a failed suicide attempt of my own brought my story full circle. You may wonder what difference the phone call made.

It allowed me to grasp just one more piece of my sanity. I was able to confirm that I'm not just some angry, unprofessional, sensitive Black woman who wants special treatment and handouts. It affirmed the gut feelings that I had and continue to have as I attempt to navigate through a society that normalizes and accepts white privilege. It allows me to demonstrate one more scenario that just might make someone drop their negative opinions and actually listen to what I have to say, to what we have to say.

May we continue to be validated and vindicated until the right people finally listen and take appropriate and consistent action. It is beyond time to dismantle the systems that are currently in place. People like me should no longer have to suffer needlessly while attempting to flourish within corporate America.

Author's Note

Thank you for lending me your ear. Putting my stories on paper has been one the most cathartic experiences of my life. Through the writing of this book, I've grown in ways unimaginable. I am now a lot gentler with and trusting of myself.

This Book Has Changed Me for The Better

When I started writing this book, I was doing it to establish myself as an expert in the workplace diversity, equity, and inclusion sector. My goal was to land more speaking engagements and consulting roles. I would do the bare minimum just so that I could say that I was a published author within this space. Little did I know that this would become such a huge message for so many, so fast. Whenever I would mention the book and my goals, people lit up with excitement, which then caused me to get more excited and to take the task a lot more seriously than I ever imagined I would.

I have recently taken time to revisit each chapter. I love myself so much more, having truly read through while recounting the inferno that I walked through in pursuit of a decent living for myself. I can finally rest in knowing that despite how egregious the encounters were, they were very much real and took a toll on my mental well-being, self-esteem, and financial health to name a few.

I write this message as a self-assured woman. Recently, I realized that not only is this book addressing some very controversial issues, it is also filled with forward confrontation. I am prepared to be met with objections and people that will attempt to discredit me. This part of the journey will aid in keeping me hungry for knowledge, passionate about the stories of others that continue to struggle, and eager to continue pounding the pavement in pursuit of anyone with power and influence that will listen.

How You Can Support Me

If there is anything that I've said that has resonated with you, I truly want to hear from you. Reach out on social media. Each of your likes, comments, and shares help the book reach more people, therefore changing more lives. If you are a leader, or have influence or authority, in regard to the equity and inclusion budget within an organization, please consider purchasing a copy of the book for the members of your team or workforce.

In addition, positive online reviews are extremely important for authors. Taking a few moments of your time to review the book on Amazon, or any other platform that you may have purchased it from would better position it through algorithms to have a greater reach out on the web.

What's Next for Me

Besides trying to find a way to finally get my photo with former President Obama, I will continue on my journey towards helping business leaders create and nurture sustainable work environments for marginalized hires.

My company offers leadership retreats, hands-on workshops and seminars, and we've recently added on-demand virtual courses that allow students to work through interactive modules at their own pace in the comfort of their own home or office.

The amount of work and change that is needed will never be done in my lifetime, but I am elated to be a part of the mighty force that works daily to make the dream of an equitable world a reality.

Cheers,

Talisa "Tali" Lavarry

Book Contributors

Kristian Ribberström:
Partner and Chief Product Officer, Medici Group

Kristian is a partner and the Chief Product Officer of The Medici Group. He focuses on their revolutionary change platform with which they activate diversity and inclusion to make teams faster, more adaptable, more collaborative, and more innovative.

His role allows him to engage with clients in a variety of industries and lead strategy sessions in twenty countries, from boardrooms in New York to tribal villages in India and Malawi. He has also spoken about diversity, inclusion, and innovation on many occasions, at such places as IMF, DOW, The World Bank, Blackstone, AstraZeneca, and TEDx to name a few.

Some clients that he has worked with are Mastercard, Disney, the European Union, Merck, ESPN, Nike, McCormick, Biogen, WWF, Under Armour, the Departmentt of Tourism for the Cayman Islands, Synchrony, and Metlife.

Colin Stokes:
TedX Speaker and Director of Communication,
Outreach and Engagement for METCO

Colin uses communications strategies to make social change—in organizations, in media, and in his own family. Elevating the voices of diverse people, he uses the principles and tools of storytelling to fight inequity and build a more just society.

He is also a public speaker and blogger on popular culture, parenting, and being a straight, white male. His TEDxBeaconStreet talks have been viewed more than 2.5 million times, including in high school and college classrooms around the world. He has spoken and facilitated dialogues in community centers, prep schools, and Walt Disney Animation Studios. He worked with LeanIn.org and Girl Scouts of America's Ban Bossy campaign to adapt the talk "How Movies Teach Manhood" into a family toolkit for starting discussions with kids about gender bias in media.

His first career was as a stage actor, specializing in musicals and Shakespeare. His background is in graphic design, Star Wars trivia, and white privilege.

Ryan Hayden:
Principal, PwC

Ryan Hayden is a Principal at PwC. He spends most of his time navigating the intersection of big technology changes and the antiquated healthcare industry. He has been in healthcare his entire life and calls himself as a data geek at heart. Ryan inspires his clients to think bigger about ways technology can improve their work life balance and deliver to their bottom lines.

He is the proud father to Taj and Niam and Husband to Rekha.

He is also an avid sports fan and kitesurfing enthusiast.

Ryan is constantly seeking ways to connect with people on a more personal level. Finding out what motivates people while encouraging them to think about ways to improve their relationships with family, friends, co-workers, and others, and to consider what their legacy will be is where he always strives to steer the conversation.

Terri Swain:
CEO, The HR Consultant

Terri Swain is the CEO of The HR Consultant in Fort Worth, TX. Operating as a Sr. Human Resources professional for multiple clients allows her to easily converse with all levels within an organization. She takes a very practical approach when managing Equal Employment Opportunity and Affirmative Action risks while keeping her clients compliant. Her expertise is successfully assisting clients through Office of Federal Contract Compliance Programs audits and setting up compliant Affirmative Action Plans.

Having worked compliance issues from the government investigation side (as an EEOC investigator), the Fortune 200 side (as an HR leader), and the consulting side with many industries, Terri offers best practices and a well-rounded approach to any table that she is seated at.

Sources

1. National Opinion Research Center at the University of Chicago's Center for Talent Innovation, *Being Black In Corporate America: An Intersectional Exploration*, National Opinion Research Center at the University of Chicago, https://www.talentinnovation.org/_private/assets/BeingBlack-KeyFindings-CTI.pdf.

2. Marianne Bertrand and Sendhil Mullainathan, "Are Emily and Greg More Employable Than Lakisha and Jamal? A Field Experiment on Labor Market Discrimination," *The American Economic Review*, 94 (4) (2004): 991–1013, available at https://cos.gatech.edu/facultyres/Diversity_Studies/Bertrand_LakishaJamal.pdf.

3. Curtis Bunn, "Blacks in Corporate America Still Largely Invisible, Study Finds," *NBC News*, Dec 11, 2019, https://www.nbcnews.com/nbcblk/blacks-corporate-america-still-largely-invisible-study-finds-n1098981.

4. Regents of the University of California v. Bakke, 438 U.S. 256 (1978).

5. Robert A. Gross, "Culture and Cultivation: Agriculture and Society in Thoreau's Concord." The Journal of American History 69, no. 1 (1982): 42-61. Accessed July 31, 2020 doi:10.2307/1887751.

CPSIA information can be obtained
at www.ICGtesting.com
Printed in the USA
LVHW041920220721
693425LV00008B/1202